Ruskin Bond's *Desh*

Ruskin Bond's *Desh*

Celebrating Root and Defining Identity

Arup Pal

BLOOMSBURY
NEW DELHI • LONDON • OXFORD • NEW YORK • SYDNEY

BLOOMSBURY INDIA
Bloomsbury Publishing India Pvt. Ltd
Second Floor, LSC Building No. 4, DDA Complex, Pocket C – 6 & 7,
Vasant Kunj, New Delhi 110070

BLOOMSBURY, BLOOMSBURY ACADEMIC INDIA and the Diana logo are trademarks of Bloomsbury Publishing Plc

First published in India 2020
This edition published 2020

Bloomsbury Academic
An imprint of Bloomsbury Publishing Plc

ISBN: HB: 978-93-88912-99-0; eBook: 978-93-89000-01-6

2 4 6 8 10 9 7 5 3 1

Typeset in Minion Pro by Manipal Technologies Limited
Printed and bound in Replika Press Pvt. Ltd.

Contents

Foreword

Arup Pal's critical appreciation of Ruskin Bond furthers the research on Bondian scholarship by offering a unique point of view. The five or so full-length critical works by different scholars on Ruskin Bond published thus far, with one exception, have mainly focused on analysing the literary achievements of the author and the influence of his personal experiences and historical time period on his creative output. However, Arup Pal's *Ruskin Bond's* Desh*: Celebrating Root and Defining Identity* focuses on four key literary works of Bond from the perspective of the author's developing sense of personal, national and cultural identity.

Based on the premise that Ruskin Bond is of mixed Indian and British ancestry—although in his interviews with me Ruskin was ambiguous (or unsure) of the racial intermixing of his ancestors during the British Raj—Arup Pal has drawn his conclusion from a thorough scrutiny of Bond's writings and the history and evolution of Anglo-Indians. This detailed analysis convinced him that Ruskin Bond indeed has a mixed racial heritage from his mother's side. It is in this sense that Arup Pal interprets the term 'Anglo-Indian' as it applies to Bond—that is, an ethnic category that emerged from interracial marriages/relationships at the time of India's colonisation by the British.

Given Arup Pal's stance and his in-depth presentation of Bond's dual heritage, *Ruskin Bond's* Desh*: Celebrating Root and Defining Identity* explores the dilemma of Bond's 'two selves' and his existential search for an identity. This discussion, analysed in six chapters, is informed by a variety of postcolonial, historical, informational and critical texts on Bond and Anglo-Indians. Arup Pal traces the journey that the author and his protagonists embark on in order to seek and ultimately define their sense of being. In presenting the author's progression from a dual Anglo-Indian identity to one that is purely Indian is juxtaposed with Ruskin Bond's personal experiences and autobiographical writings.

In exploring Bond's inner search for an identity, Arup Pal does not analyse the works in order of publication; rather, he adopts a thematic approach by first establishing Bond's upbringing and lifestyle in colonial India and during the early years of Indian independence. He begins with *Scenes from a Writer's Life: A Memoir*, which is a collection of Bond's journal entries, partial autobiography, copies of letters written to him, photographs and personal notes spanning the first 21 years of his life; this time period covers Bond's childhood and schooling in India and ends with his return to Dehradun with a book contract in hand after spending four years in Britain. Published in 1997, *Scenes from a Writer's Life: A Memoir* describes the economic, social, cultural, family, and political uniqueness of Anglo-Indians and provides background information on the choices that they—hence Ruskin Bond—had to make, or the options open to them, when the British Raj was dismantled. Pal's research is thorough and provides a sympathetic and detailed background to the plight of Anglo-Indians prior to and after Indian independence. The next chapter goes back chronologically to Bond's first publication, *The Room on the Roof* (1956), written in Britain when he was only 17. Arup Pal argues, in Chapter 3, that the adolescent author sensitively presents the inner trauma of the protagonist, Rusty, who ultimately resolves his identity crisis by 'decolonising his mind'. Pal depicts the Anglo-Indian world view and the adolescent author's aversion to colonial prejudices and a clear preference for Indian friends and culture. He further attributes the freedom and individuality of Bond's attitude to his experience of studying in the midst of the Himalayan mountains and to his father's accepting personality and teachings; hence, the resulting sense of cultural dislocation and feeling of loss during Bond's brief sojourn in Britain makes him realise that India is his home and where he belongs. Pal emphasises that Bond's early works do not reveal a colonial attitude; instead, they portray him as a sensitive Anglo-Indian who is caught in the 'double-bind' of his heritage.

In the chapter on *A Flight of Pigeons* (published in book form in 1980), Arup Pal argues that Ruskin Bond identifies with Miriam Labrador, the female protagonist of this historical novel set in Shahjahanpur during the war of 1857, which was fought by Indian *sepoys* seeking independence from the British army. Again, based on thorough background research and taking a sympathetic stance, Pal states that Anglo-Indians were twice marginalised—first by the British and then by Indians. He portrays the pain and terror experienced by a mixed-race Christian mother during the 'Mutiny' by examining the character of Miriam, not from the perspective of the war, but as one who is knowledgeable of and sympathetic towards Muslim–Indian culture, noting how she successfully bridges the cultural divide—and thus survives. Pal points out that this cross-cultural amalgamation is obvious not only in Miriam's physical features but also in her knowledge of Muslim culture.

Arup Pal comes full circle with *A Handful of Nuts* by structurally integrating this chapter with the ones that went before it. He emphasises that the novel evokes a time when Bond was much younger and his beloved Dehradun still exuded a relaxed small-town atmosphere, revealing its 'sentiments, superstitions, biases, failures, and aspirations'. Published in 1996, when the author was 62, the unnamed first-person narrator has already resolved his identity crisis and is comfortable with his 'belongingness to India'. Far from rebelling against his British background, the 21-year-old protagonist (and by extension the author) has completely assimilated the overarching culture and subcultures of Dehradun. Indeed, Dehradun is a microcosm of India, and in evoking its past and the author's younger self, Pal notes that both the novelist and his protagonist have achieved a 'liberal Indian consciousness'.

From the perspective of literary criticism, Pal's selection of books discussed here explores how Bond progresses as a writer and a thinker. The creative distance necessary in writing these books helps not only to resolve the identity crisis of Bond's protagonists but of Bond as well. Pal's selection of works, where either Bond or his protagonists are between the ages of 17 and 21, is significant. As we learn from developmental psychologists these are formative years in an adolescent's or young adult's life, but especially in Bond's, given the dilemma of his 'two selves', his parents' divorce and mother's remarriage to a Punjabi businessman, his father's early death, and his move to Britain and eventual return to the Himalayan mountains. While the above works were not written in chronological order, Arup Pal's thematic structure gives Bond's mixed-race struggles a sense of coherence by first focusing on his biographical background, then discussing an adolescent novel that explores issues of identity, and next interrogating how one can be both Anglo and Indian through a female protagonist. Finally, after returning to India and settling in the mountains, Ruskin knew that he was 'home' and that India was where he belonged. Even though one continues to evolve throughout life, Arup Pal points out that it is from the strength of knowing who he is on the inside that Ruskin Bond finds the answer to his question, 'Where do I belong?' There is no longer a clash between his British and Indian selves in post-independent India; instead, there is a happy blend of both in the multicultural lifestyle and world view of the author.

I congratulate Arup Pal on the publication of *Ruskin Bond's* Desh*: Celebrating Root and Defining Identity* and for its examination of Ruskin Bond's journey in search of his inner self with a depth of understanding and historical insight.

Meena G. Khorana, PhD
Professor of English and Adolescent Literature (Retired)
Department of English and Language Arts
Morgan State University
Baltimore, Maryland, USA

Preface

Ruskin Bond's Desh: *Celebrating Root and Defining Identity* explores Bond's evolving identity that finds expression in his oeuvre. While writing this book, I meander through Anglo-Indian history, Indian colonial and nationalist politics, the author's personal and familial space and postcolonial connotations of home and exile. In order to grasp Bond's evolving self, I refrain from maintaining a sequential progress; the study is rather based on the thematic approach of Bond's self-making while negotiating the sociocultural and political backdrop of the Anglo-Indian community in India. My understanding is also based on a close scrutiny of biographical information found in Bond's memoirs, Professor Meena G. Khorana's biographical research (2003) and on three personal interviews taken at Bond's residence in Landour.

An Indian author of British descent, Ruskin Bond is one of the major figures in the Indian literary scene. Yet, he has long been neglected in serious literary discourse because of his penchant for apparently simple story-telling and autobiographical discourse. Even though Bond won the Indian Council for Child Education Award for his crucial role in the development of children's literature in India in 1987 and the Sahitya Akademi Award for his book *Our Trees Still Grow in Dehra* in 1992, it is only recently that he has earned critical acclaim for the sophistication of his art of story-telling. Ruskin Bond has shown that writing can at once be lucid and thought-provoking, direct and compelling. In his semi-autobiographical oeuvre, one can notice that Bond, the author is often unidentifiable with Bond, the person. The biographical history provided in this study is therefore relevant. One realises that the idea of the authorial 'self' is remarkably present in Bond's fictional selves, perhaps because the author wishes to see the world from an intimate perspective and to measure himself by fictionalising personal desires. In this exists a quest for identity—a yearning for individuation. To understand this, the present study progresses through questioning, critiquing and explaining this individual journey. The book concentrates on the idea that an Anglo-Indian is also an Indian, and traces a slow but certain transition of Bond's authorial self from the existential concern experienced in the formative years of the author to the developing consciousness of his mature years.

We realise that Ruskin Bond's literary output is the celebration of a developing 'self'—from being merely an 'Anglo-Indian' to an Indian. To explain this, the present study is divided into six chapters dealing with four major texts. While in the introductory chapter, a contextual reading of Anglo-Indian self-identification and self-definition in post-independent India is addressed, the second chapter on his journal *Scenes* is studied as a site of personal awakening. The chapter on *The Room on the Roof* inquires how the developing awareness of Bond's fictional self-helps him overcome colonial biases. Chapter 4 is an enunciation of liberal India, where a person of mixed-descent can effortlessly mingle with other Indians amidst thousands of differences without any moral obligation; a cross-cultural and cross-racial intersection is proposed here. How one's familial space nurtures and ascertains one's belongingness is advocated in Chapter 5. Here Bond's role often shifts from that of a novelist to a memoirist, rendering an intimate understanding of a space that makes him who he is. This is followed by the concluding chapter proffering how Ruskin Bond identifies himself outside racial or politicised affiliation. The identity-dilemma due to his quasi-Indianness is subverted by his keen awareness of himself as an individual.

One cannot deny the intricate, and often confusing, Anglo-Indian history while evaluating someone who is, by origin, a member of the community. Ruskin Bond's way to seeing beyond his position in 'Anglo-Indian'–'Indian' identity generates the thesis of this book. Although Bond's positioning is complicated due to his 'double-bind', his adolescent self seems to know how to overcome it. My understanding of Bond's way of seeing may be different from that of another. In that case, I look forward to understanding how that disagreement responds to this approach.

Acknowledgements

Without *Roads to Mussoorie* (2005), an easily overlooked non-fiction by Ruskin Bond, my research and consequently, this book would never have been written. On a bustling winter afternoon, I bought it from the Rupa Stall at the Kolkata Book Fair, 2014. Upon reading it, I found that its author had written a Backward instead of a Foreword because, as the author notes, it suited his personality. Intrigued by this deviation of the author from standard practice, I became deeply interested in his personal history. Albeit in an unusual fashion, the seeds of my interest in Ruskin Bond had been sown.

The initial idea of this study germinated through an exchange of ideas with my teacher, Dr Samrat Laskar, in 2014. The project was further developed with some critical insights by Dr Saurav Dasthakur, Department of English, Visva-Bharati. Professor Nandini Bhattacharya and Dr Subhajit Sen Gupta, two of my external experts from the University of Burdwan, encouraged me to turn my doctoral thesis into a monograph. Professor Debashis Bandyopadhyay's scholarship on Bond has enriched my understanding too. I appreciate and am deeply grateful for their support.

I am particularly thankful to R. Chandra Sekhar of Bloomsbury India for his immediate interest and enthusiasm about this project. Many thanks are due to my anonymous reviewer for his perceptive suggestions and criticism, and to the entire editorial team of Bloomsbury. I would like to thank my supervisor, Professor Goutam Ghosal, for his guidance and for the degree of freedom that he so readily granted during my doctoral research. I am also thankful to the generous Department of English, Visva-Bharati, for allowing space for new ideas. I express my gratitude to Sumana Roy, whom I personally consider one of the finest essayists of today, for her constant encouragement. I take this opportunity to especially thank Dr Shrabani Basu for helping me structure the manuscript.

I am fortunate to have received the encouragement of Professor Meena G. Khorana, Ruskin Bond's literary biographer, who has written the Foreword for this book. Her continuous support and abiding interest in this subject helped me immensely. I would also like to express my gratitude to all my teachers at the Department of English, Visva-Bharati, especially to Professor Amrit Sen, to Dr Sudev Pratim Basu and to Dr Dipankar Roy. I am thankful to Dr Robyn Andrews and Brent Howitt Otto, the editors of the *International Journal of Anglo-Indian Studies*. Thanks are also due to The National Library, Kolkata, to *The Derozio Anglo-Indian Research Collection* at the Central Library, University of Calcutta and to the Central Library of Visva-Bharati.

Ruskin Bond, Professor Meena G. Khorana and Professor Ganesh Saili have been affectionate and somewhat indulgent to a precocious scholar throughout the writing of this book. This is the time to acknowledge their selfless responses to my 'bookish' queries and doubts.

And to my parents and my sister—who have stood by, ready to support whenever I stumbled—I dedicate all my love.

Arup Pal

Kolkata, August 2019

1

The Idea of the Self

Identity, Hyphenation and Problems of Definition

Born in Kasauli, Himachal Pradesh, Ruskin Bond—novelist, memoirist, essayist, short-story writer and poet, now best known for his contribution to children's literature in India—grew up in Jamnagar, Dehradun and Shimla (Simla) before settling in Landour, Mussoorie.[1] When Bond was born to Aubrey Alexander Bond and Edith Clerke in 1934, he was unaware of the colonial rhetoric through which his identity was to be fashioned. Before he fully realised his nationality, he had to negotiate the politically and culturally charged social location of his mixed-racial origin. Although Bond bears within him British blood, he has hardly approached his subject from this perspective.[2] The curiosity in understanding the nature of reality, which is evident in some of his initial works, is due to an adolescent impulse and sensitivity towards the subject. The expression 'Anglo-Indian'[3] used in this study should not be confused with that of the British residents in India; it is employed to mean a mixed European and Indian identity. This book is also not an attempt to trace postcolonial Anglo-Indian identity in general; nor does it intend to examine the British political agenda behind the hyphenation of mixed-descent. It is focused primarily on Ruskin Bond's (Anglo-) Indian self and how it fits into the cultural fabric of post-independent India. I trace a slow but certain transition from psychological anxiety experienced by the authorial self in his formative years due to 'a complex of factors referable to the colonial past' (Caplan 2001, 11) to a developing consciousness of maturer years. Since Bond's works are semi-autobiographical, a synonymous shift from the vexation of the double-bind to an understanding as a free Indian national is reflected in his fictional representations. A change of perspective is discernible, where the author's concern is no longer limited to issues like Anglo-Indian existential angst or debates on the extent of Indianness of an Anglo-Indian.

As a child of rapidly changing times, Bond was brought up with a secular world view. His father never discouraged him to socialise with other Indians outside their community. In fact, he spent the first five years with other children in the princely state of Jamnagar where Aubrey Bond was appointed as a tutor-guardian. It is here that infant Bond was 'more exposed to Indian culture than the average British child in India' (Khorana 2003, 8). The aesthetic sense that Ruskin Bond owns came primarily from his father and partially from how he was affected by his surroundings.[4] Speaking of how environs act as shaping agent, Bond says:

> I chose the hills for the purpose of *living* rather than as a congenial place for writing. The mountains make a man realize just how insignificant he is. At the same time, they allow one to remain an individual instead of being swallowed in the crowd. (2001, x)

In a personal interview, Bond told me[5] that he hardly remembers any British friend who had been close to his father. However, in *The Room of Many Colours*, the adolescent authorial identity, whose set of ideas was indirectly shaped by the ruling British, is confused at his father's intent to return to England—the assumed 'home' of Anglo-Indians. The schismatic self of the young Bond now encounters questions about his true belonging: Is not India his native land? Who are Anglo-Indians then? Are they essentially Europeans with some Indian blood, or are their identical roots determined solely by European blood? Are they more 'Anglo' than 'Indian'? Where do they actually belong, or, where is their original 'home'? Can their ancestral root be dubbed as their motherland? How far is the age-old concept that 'England is home' justifiable today? Have their dual-inheritance been fruitful in terms of reinforcing their sociocultural acceptance in India? Or, are they really not Indians?

Indian colonial history recounts that Anglo-Indians are of British (or European) descent and the result of British colonialism in India. However, the British in India often ignored their identity. The disquiet of Anglo-Indians due to the British political agenda in colonial India has long been debated: 'The British frequently viewed them stereotypically as Indians with some European blood; the Indians often considered them Europeans with some Indian blood' (Gist and Wright 1973, 152). The British did not favour this minority community because the former wanted to retain their superiority to the latter, while the Anglo-Indians' constant moral support added to their assistance to the British force in some of the significant political moves against colonised India sowed the seed of mistrust among the 'natives' (Muthiah 2013, 40). Such rejection—both by the British and the Indians—engendered an identity trauma that widened the sociocultural schism of Anglo-Indians on the one hand, while on the other, their lifestyle, religion, outlook, practice, dress-code, language and English customs made them socially and culturally alienated from the native Indians. In their study, N.P. Gist and R.D. Wright mention that '[t]he prejudices against them, real or imagined, or the prejudices that they themselves may hold against other Indians', were 'an obstacle to both group and individual identity' (ibid., 55). Under such dual reception, they were suspended in a liminal space. This consequently gave rise to a fervent quest for national identity among the Anglo-Indians in post-independent India. Their status is further complicated because, despite their Indian root and nationality, they are often culturally inclined towards the West. Let us see, for instance, how they are received by the Constitution of India. In Article 366, Section 2, they are defined thus:

> "[A]n Anglo-Indian" means a person whose father or any of whose other male progenitors in the male line is or was of European descent but who is domiciled within the territory of India and is or was born

> within such territory of parents habitually resident therein and not established there for temporary purposes only [. . . .] (155)

This ('gender-biased') definition often turns out to be a riddle considering their obvious/partial Indian origin. In addition, since the colonial history of India has made the Anglo-Indian a politicised identity, the Anglo-Indian communal distinctiveness has been conditioned and misinterpreted by innumerable reasons. One must remember that the British policy in colonial India encouraged European men to marry native women. Those who had come to serve in India, naturally, built liaisons with their maids or with other Indian women. This strengthened the British disregard of them. In other words, the British took this opportunity to tag them as 'half-caste'. Although the Anglo-Indians are of 'European descent in the male line of mixed European and Indian blood' (Anthony 1969, 3), they have been considered by-products of a British imperial policy to rule India better. By the 19th century, to their befuddlement, the British categorised fairer and wealthier mixed-blood people as 'Anglo-Indian' and darker ones as 'Eurasians' (James 2003, 52). It was since the 1911 census, after Lord Hardinge's act (Moore 1996, 51), that the term 'Eurasians' was modified as Anglo-Indians, while their underlying dilemma for identity continued to exist for an unspecific extent of time.

The liminality of Anglo-Indians started deteriorating in the 1940s, especially towards the end of the decade. Blair Williams, an Anglo-Indian scholar, registers this in his study of the community:

> Throughout their history they tried to assimilate into the English mainstream, but the English rejected them. The Anglo-Indians (on the other hand) did not accept their Indian heritage, tending to look down on Indians of other communities. This approach of theirs caused Indian communities to resent them and in turn, isolated them from the rest of India. And so the Community lived for over two hundred years of British rule not being accepted by either the British or the Indians. (Muthiah and MacLure 2013, 102–03)

Such an idea of segregation is echoed in literature too. In 1978, noted novelist Stephen Alter published his first novel *Neglected Lives* on the ageing and isolated Anglo-Indian community in a fictional hill town of Debrakot. The narrative tone is elegiac and sensitive. We are introduced to Theodore Augden, a narrator of mixed-descent, commenting on his community's predicament of the 1940s:

> Partition, 1947, the English let India slip out of their hands and it broke in two. It was a period of allegiance and hatred. Pride was the emotion of the time and everyone felt kinship to their own race, their own religion, their own families. The politicians were pulled apart, the army was severed, and sides had to be taken.
>
> For us it was a period of confusion; the English abandoned us, not that they had really ever cared who we were or what happened to us. (2008, 42)

Debrakot can be sensed in the insularity of the European community of Dehradun in Ruskin Bond's *The Room on the Roof* (1956), but one also notices a dissimilar perspective in narrative treatment. Whereas Alter's tale seems to have immersed into the mixed-blood dilemma in an isolated terrain; Bond's narrative (discussed in Chapter 3), seems to depart from the 'ageing Anglo-Indian community'.

Written in the context of the 1940s, with socioeconomic insecurity looming large among the community, Patrick Taylor, one of the three narrators and an Anglo-Indian railwayman in John Masters's 1954 novel *Bhowani Junction*, sighs: '[W]e couldn't go Home. We couldn't become English, because we were half Indian. We couldn't become Indian, because we were half English. We could only stay where we were and be what we were' (27–28). Masters' Anglo-Indian characters could not see India other than an alien sky, which appears as a constant reminder to underpin their inability to find a home in the subcontinent and to overcome racial identification. They were torn apart trying to decide which group between Indian and British was their own. Their search for an ideal abode, where the liberating sense of seeing themselves as a Western-inclined identity in a relatable geographical boundary, met with an unfulfilling outcome.

While commenting on the preceding decade, Kuntala Lahiri-Dutt informs us that '[t]he impending departure of the British from India generated a sense of betrayal and insecurity' in the 1930s among the Anglo-Indians who then must look for new ways for survival and depend less on the government (2013, n.pag.). Even when they were given legal citizenship of India, facilitating their presence in the job market by the 1935 Act, Indian 'natives' continued to treat them as British subjects with respect to education and internal security. This induced the idea for a separate homeland. Their utopian search for a home, however, was no longer possible because England or any other European country could hardly substitute their concept of home—an idea without neglecting one's emotional space. They, however, managed to buy about 10,000 acres of land in 1933 near Ranchi (now in Jharkhand) in Chotanagpur under the leadership of E.T. McCluskie. McCluskieganj shortly came alive with a distinctive lifestyle of the Anglo-Indian settlers, but it was with the demise of their leader that this utopian concept failed miserably.

In *The Trotter Nama* (1988), Anglo-Indian author Irwin Allan Sealy fictionalises (and historicises) this predicament:

> The Hindus wanted theirs, the Muslims wanted theirs, the British were going back to theirs. What about us? [. . .] A place for those who were neither Indian nor European, who spoke English and ate curries with a spoon. [. . .] And yet he too wanted a home. He was only half at home here. Could one have a home that one had never been to, that filled one's chest with a prickly longing, like the plainsman's longing for the mountains he had never known? (491–92)

It is indeed that Indian colonial history not only trapped them between British ignorance and Indian nationalist idiom but also widened their anguish. As V.P. Anvar Sadath argues:

> Most of these representations of the Anglo-Indians as an ethnicity apparently derived their initial inspiration from the community's complex origin and hybrid status, and therefore they looked at the members of the community as 'orphans' of colonialism, thus

considering them as people with a not-so-impressive racial standing. (quoted in Peppin 2012, xi)

In his study, Bryan Peppin begins his argument with these witty observations to question the stereotyped notions through which an Anglo-Indian is seen as a non-Indian. He states that an Anglo-Indian is essentially an Indian. There are valid reasons behind his claim: first, since Anglo-Indians are quasi-Indian from their maternal connection, they cannot be identified as non-Indians; second, had the origin of their community not been materialised in India, the underlying question regarding their existence and consequent dilemma would hardly have any ground.

In post-independent India, however, Anglo-Indian existence is not limited to the 'Indian'/'Anglo-Indian' binary; rather it is almost indistinguishable from other Indians. Among the Anglo-Indians who are protective to retain their ethnicity are willing to be known as representatives of the community. In contrary, there are people who are reluctant to be identified with communal identity. In this book, I shall be concerned with the second predilection. I would like to study whether Ruskin Bond's sense of belonging to India makes his politicised identity insignificant, or if his stance critiques any rigid definition of that. In this ongoing section, a contextual reading of Anglo-Indian self-identification and self-definition in post-independent India is addressed.

An Anglo-Indian's Search for Indianness

Ruskin Bond's body of works, which can be studied as an enquiry into Anglo-Indian identity, also questions their problematic equation with Indian national identity. To say that Bond's world is not limited to Anglo-Indian communal expression does not simply suggest any denial of their idea of 'becoming Indian'. This complication comes from the idea of foreignness embedded in the identity. The concept of foreignness, or what once popularly and often negatively was called *firangi*, is in fact associated with the word 'India', which 'derived from the Greek name for a river in what is now Pakistan—the Indus' (Harris 2015, 285). While clarifying his concept 'becoming Indian', Jonathan Gil Harris argues for many 'Indiannesses' on the basis of the economic, social and cultural, and proposes that the authenticity of Indianness is possible through simultaneous amalgamation of the local and the foreign: 'the "Indian" is always becoming something new, and is constantly being renegotiated and transformed in a multitude of ways, because of unexpected conversations between local traditions and foreign elements' (ibid., 286). It is among the many understandings of Indian identity due to multiple border-crossings; I try to explain an Anglo-Indian's Indian consciousness in terms of wider cultural currents, where the insistence of gliding away from the immediate demarcation of a racially hybrid minority to India's diversifying possibilities is also true. Bond's idea of conceptualising the Anglo-Indian consciousness, based on the premise, can be extended with what Ernest Renan once stated: 'Let us not abandon the fundamental principle that man is a reasonable and moral being, before he is cooped up in such and such a language, before he is a member of such and such a race, before he belongs to such and such a culture' (1990, 17).

Such understanding of assimilating liberal ideas of oneness was evident in the poetry of Henry Louis Vivian Derozio (1809–31), the first national poet of India. It would, therefore, be interesting to see, as we proceed with this present discussion, how Ruskin Bond's double-inheritance circuitously comments on his root in India. Unlike many noted mixed-blood writers, Derozio and Bond could liberate themselves in their views in understanding India. Rudyard Kipling (1865–1936), though not of racial mix, but an Anglo-Indian according to colonial connotation, wrote the following in *The Ballad of East and West*: 'East is East, and West is West, and never the twain shall meet...' (27). Although English novelist E.M. Forster (1879–1970) overcame Kipling's imperialist viewpoint in his 1924 novel *A Passage to India*, he was stuck in the riddle of the Malabar Caves. In 1954, when Ruskin Bond reverted to India after his brief exile to Britain to establish his literary career with renewed faith, John Masters's *Bhowani Junction*, dealing with the Anglo-Indian community's exodus, was published. In this context, it is indeed not the point of validation whether or to what extent a work of art could represent a community's desire. Rather, the argument should be advanced with the authorial choice. In his novelistic saga *The Trotter Nama*, Irwin Allan Sealy feels the urgency to voice the proud existence of an Anglo-Indian communal identity in postcolonial India, as if writing back to the Empire in sarcastic humour. He, however, leaves his tale open-ended. Sealy, who appears to be a little protective of his mixed-descent, seems to restore the individualist choice of an Anglo-Indian in double-inheritance. Sealy, despite the racial connotation, is an Indian. But Sealy's Indianness is reflected by reinforcing his Anglo-Indianness as a minority—not as a binary to majority, but essentially as a part of Indian's diversifying spirit. What I mean is that Sealy consciously retains his communal distinctiveness in order to be an Indian.

Ruskin Bond, who had already anticipated the individual need by dissenting his liminal consciousness as early as at the age of seventeen, conceived *The Room on the Roof* (henceforth *The Room* in this chapter) in the 1950s. But, Bond does not shy away to present the identity dilemma of Rusty, where Rusty's vexation due to divided loyalties constitutes critical turns. In Bond's vision, the slim line of Anglo-Indian protectiveness gradually dissolves somewhere with the intent by which an individual, despite racial differences, identifies with everyday Indianness. In other words, if we closely study Bond's Anglo-Indian characterisation in general, we come to a point where the boundary between an 'Indian' and an 'Anglo-Indian' is diffused. This is probably because he wishes his Anglo-Indian characters not to be recognisable in liminal terms. Of course, the vacillation cannot be overlooked, but he really does not wish to see them particularly as domiciled Europeans in India. As opposed to Eurocentric biases, Rusty, the fictional representation of the novelist, is emotionally connected to the Indian environment even though he is culturally inclined towards the West. Going beyond the racial stereotypes of his community, the adolescent protagonist's endless search for selfhood (in *The Room*) is achieved, the text suggests, through decolonising the mind. Rusty is imagined essentially as an Indian identity and thus not written from an Anglo-Indian standpoint. Rusty's act of becoming Indian is possible at his refusal to succumb to his guardian's private world of thoughts—'pureness', and to emerge as a secular identity in Dehra's eclecticism. Another significant aspect to note is that rather than being identified solely from any racial purview, Bond's alter-ego sees India as his *desh*, a native place, where he rightfully belongs amidst thousands of differences without bothering about his racial, religious and communal affiliations. In other words, the novelist has not measured Rusty's identity by his descent, but by his will. In his autobiography *Lone Fox Dancing* (2017), Bond confirms:

> I am not one of those who look up their family trees in order to discover that a great-grandmother was related to the Czar of Russia and that a great-granduncle was probably Queen Victoria's lover. I am happy to accept that Grandfather Bond was a good soldier (he retired as drill sergeant) and that Grandfather Clerke (my mother's father) helped in the making of solid railway carriages for the Northern Railway. (10)

The main reason, why in spite of an English upbringing Ruskin Bond manages an inside Indian viewpoint, lies in his outlook, which remains free from colonial affiliation.

Life Follows No Plot

Bond's writing exhilarates in unravelling the adolescent psyche. Under a deceptively simple manner, he reaches the psyche of the human soul—be it the suppressed desire of a child, or the angst of a mixed-blood, or the joy of a Garhwali. It is his simplicity that lends conviction to his sincerity as an artist. In *A Book of Simple Living* (2015), he outlines his creative theory:

> As in life, so in art: only connect. I have always believed that to communicate and be readable is all that a writer should aim for. People ask me why my style is so simple. I think it is because I want my readers to feel what I feel, to see what I see, and big words and big sentences get in the way of this sharing. It is clarity and honesty that I am striving to attain; there can be no lasting connection with my readers without these. And to be clear and open is to be simple. (122)

Bond's frame of mind enables him to employ thoughts in comprehensible terms. When, therefore, he is questioned of being 'too lucid' (and sometimes repetitive), we are reminded that his primary aim is to 'communicate' and 'to be loyal' to the readers. Bond's earnestness for truthful communication insinuates his concern to actively engage his readers with what he has to offer in his writerly journey of self-discovery. Bond's refusal (or failure) to limit himself while ideating his protagonist emerges from this promise of loyalty in the 'act of communication' with his readers. It is not unlikely to think that when he tells a story, he appears to be a part of it. Sometimes, the fine line between the fictional self and the author-persona trespasses unhesitatingly. Consider Rusty's self-questioning at his hasty decision about leaving India in *The Room*: 'What I am saying [I do not belong here], thought Rusty, why do I make my inheritance a justification for my present bitterness? No one has cast me out . . . of my own free will I want to run away from India . . . why do I blame inheritance?' (91). It is directly relatable to the adolescent memoirist's vacillation, presented in the form of diary entries in *Scenes from a Writer's Life* (2012), in pursuit of procuring literary fame in Britain:

> I can write here—anywhere—but it is the desire for recognition and applause that lures me away. I tell myself that fame is not greatness, and that if I remain as I am long enough I shall soon grow accustomed to obscurity. At least I shall retain my *individuality, and in art that is most important*. (359; emphasis mine)

Again, just like Rusty, the author-persona turns out to be the only young representative of Dehra's domiciled European community (333). One can, therefore, anticipate that what the author opines is well resonated in his fictional representation. Part of such inquiry lies in *The Room*, his magnum opus; the art of transcending reality into fiction or vice versa is taken care of in later works as well, but hardly any of his works can rival the truthfulness and emotive outbursts shown here. In the introduction to *The Night Train at Deoli and Other Stories* (1988), the same story-teller reveals: 'I can't really write unless I am in love with my subject' (9) and in self-reserved tone continues that his book may often sound autobiographical because of the incidents directly drawn from personal life: 'I am that kind of a writer, that kind of a person' (9). If this is considered to be a weakness, the same turns out to be his strength. Murli Das Melwani defends Bond's autobiographical penchant in his article:

> One criticism that may be levelled against Bond is that he puts too much of himself in his stories. But what else has a writer to offer except himself? And if the personality the writer presents is as engaging as the one Bond does, we would like more of it. (1995, 45)

Nearly each of his works crisscrosses autobiographical incidents. Why is this necessary? One could argue that Bond's act of fictionalising personal experiences is a kind of allowance in order to re-imagine the memory of himself drawing upon a kind of self-appraisal. It will be interesting to quote here a few lines from a letter, written in 1964 by Diana Athill, Bond's first literary mentor and the editor of Andre Deutsch, to the author:

> Your snag is, surely, that you are a writer who works best from very close to your own experience—which means that one is terribly dependant on the nature of one's experience. Only so much that is of general validity happens to one—and only so much of what happens to one strikes down to the level from which one writes. I sometimes feel very envious of people with the other kind of mind, full of invention. But I still like best the kind of writing which goes inwards rather than outwards. (Bond 2012, 259)

The validation of subjective intrusion as 'terrible dependence' in fictional works can at once be artistic and truthful. By casting a mind largely dependent on autobiographical elements, the novelist establishes a site for self-making. In such cases, things may not always be in his favour, but the authorial self is still very much resonant because the protagonist's (in this context, Rusty) life has already been lived upon. Thus, what Rusty introspects is most of the time Bond's own thoughts. In *A Handful of Nuts*, the narrator's act of restoring the languorous Dehra of his youth is not far removed from the author-persona's version of the 1950s Dehra. There are some factual references to real-life experiences as well, which I have elaborated in Chapter 5, and the reader seems to feel the sense of truth mutely permeated, without which Bond's merit could have been otherwise.

Narrativising Space, Opening Corridors

In Bond's literary output, the idea of 'space' plays an integral part by constituting a cultural milieu in accordance with the idiosyncrasies of his characters. When we are introduced to Dehra, we are immediately invited to its day-to-day specificities. Dehra is there but not restricted to local idiosyncrasies. This Dehra is also India—local yet liberal, small yet all-encompassing. Bond's Dehra goes beyond its Dehra-ness and creates a personal space. Dehra is written, at one point, through the lens of an adolescent, who refuses to grow up. At the other end of the spectrum, Dehra is filled with Bond's banal queries. The underlying wish to become Dehra is readily hinted almost everywhere in his oeuvre. In his brief stay in Britain, home goes missing. Britain fails to give him thrill, which Dehra fulfils. A sojourner's search for 'home' in Britain gives birth to traumatic experiences and opens up interpretative possibilities. From the motif of losing home abroad, Bond decides not to venture further. He therefore lets his fictional identity roam anywhere he likes, but not outside India, lest the idea of homing gets lost. Dehra, to the authorial identity, metonymically stands for memory, intimacy and warmth, where he can meander through chapters. I shall discuss later how, in his imagination, Dehra's '*barsati*' (literally, a room on the roof) becomes a room of his detailed interest, providing him space where one's connection is instinctively true. We shall also see how the evocation of Dehra in his foreignness is unavoidable and immediate. The reference to Dehra, as a setting, has thus re-emerged as a space to enlighten his consciousness of being in India, both physically and psychologically. One may find no 'real' activity while revealing the place of action in Bondian narrative because it refuses to distort the banal world in the name of an intellectualised approach called defamiliarisation (Chaudhuri 2018, 250). The pleasure to have intimacy with a place, almost always postcolonial, makes Bond's universe more relevant and more modern.

Talking of geographical setting, Anglo-Indian/British hill settlement in India and its consequent isolation has commonly found its entry in the works of Anglo-Indian authors: 'British society in colonial India represented an island that cultivated isolation, racial superiority, and power. [. . .] They saw no sense in belonging to India, because it was considered ill-mannered and inferior to "go native"' (Khorana 2003, 3). This sense of superiority, which Anglo-Indians owned from the British, continued to prevail post-1947. No wonder, such attitude distanced them from other Indians. But, what strikes one is that young Bond noticed such prejudices, understood their possible hindrances, and wrote a novel as a dissent to racial myth. It is striking because the refusal to succumb to racial differences comes from one who shares *métis* origin. How Ruskin Bond is capable of doing this preoccupies the central idea of this study. Kipling's stance, introduced above, resembles that of a stranger's eye, who finds himself within the superiority of the Whites. His immaculate knowledge in portraying physical India halts at his youthful fascination, which, sometimes, turns out to be a drawback. Bond's short story *The Man Who Was Kipling* (1988) begins with the narrator's concern to stress Kipling's literary genius but proceeds to comment on the latter's imperialist view. The narrator encounters Kipling's ghost in the Indian Section of the Victoria and Albert Museum in London and exonerates him for his belief that '"the Empire was [is] a fine and noble thing"' (32). The judicious reader in Bond finds that *Kim* (1901) is the outcome of Kipling's nostalgia for India and naturally contoured with the novelist's penchant to create his own world: 'A fair land—a most beautiful land is this of Hind—and the land of the Five Rivers is fairer than all' (Bond 1992, 86). Kipling's Simla (now Shimla) is what Kipling wanted it to be; one thus should not look for real-life resemblance. Bond wrote this observation in the 1960s. Later in 2012, when he revised his view in his introduction to Kipling's *Just So Stories* (reprinted by Rainlight), he, perhaps unknown to himself, still maintains an analogous view: 'These [the stories] were celebrations of India. But in them, he described India not as it was, but as he wanted it to be' (ix). Contrary to Kipling's biased self, Bond's portrayal of India dwells in lived experiences, departing sharply from exoticising the land.

An image that appears frequently in Ruskin Bond's oeuvre is his enunciation of common humanity, be it humanising the Anglo-Indian spinster in 'The Prospect of Flowers', or the old man in 'My Father's Trees in Dehra' (Bond 1988) or in portraying Mariam who, by Indian colonial history, is of mixed-descent in *A Flight of Pigeons*, not forgetting numerous Indian characters from hundreds of other tales. In *A Flight of Pigeons*, for instance, Mariam's fondness for other Indians of Shahjahanpur outside her community and her heroic endeavour to save her family during the politically charged situation enable her to see the reverse terrain of racial hostilities. While 're-imagining' Mariam (since his ideation relies on Fanthome's historical account), as late as in the 1970s, Bond is well past his initial Anglo-Indian dilemma; he perhaps finds it more relevant to present humanity in fiction, where the Indian—be it a Sikh, or a Garhwali, or an Anglo-Indian—is a humane representation in the purview of the author's imagination. For that matter, in 'The Prospect of Flowers', Miss Mackenzie, who has no relatives in India or abroad, has been living in an Indian hill station for decades. For the sake of discussion, I shall consult with another version of the story called 'It Must Be the Mountains: A Thirty-Minute Play for Radio', which had never been aired or staged before it appeared in *Rain in the Mountains* (1993). Set in the 1970s, when the number of Anglo-Indians dwindling in India witnessed its second phase, 86-year-old Miss Mackenzie lives all alone in a remote cottage called Mulberry Lodge with occasional visitors. Among them, Anil, a 12-year-old schoolboy, trespasses her garden one day and starts conversing with her, making her feel sociable. On being asked, Miss Mackenzie, based on a real person called Miss Ripley-Bean who shared Bond's Maplewood Cottage for a short time, expresses to Anil that she could not return to England because it was almost impossible for her to begin life anew at such an old age; she adds that '[m]y home is here, Anil—in these hills, among these trees', which 'take away some of the loneliness' (Bond 1996, 76). Any sensitive reader would relate the longing of Miss Mackenzie for her country to Bond's personal philosophy. This transmutation of authorial identity into that of the old woman can thus be read as an act of re-living in and with the Himalayas. The importance of the Himalayas in the author's personal quest is explained in the same journal:

> It was while I was living in England, in the jostle and drizzle of London, that I remembered the Himalayas at their most vivid. I had grown up amongst those great blue and brown mountains; they had nourished my blood; and though I was separated from them by thousands of miles of ocean, plain and desert, I could not rid them from my system. It is always the same with mountains. Once you have lived with them for any length of time, you belong to them. There is no escape. (92)

Perhaps nowhere, but in the above lines, that the love for Indian space is so finely conveyed. Apart from the Anglo-Indian old-age dilemma of emigration, Miss Mackenzie and Anil partially represent the author's two selves in dialogue—one self reassuring the other for choosing India over Britain:

> Anil: Are you going away?
> Miss M: I'm not sure.
> Anil: Are you going back to England?
> Miss M: No, I couldn't that. I'm too old to start life all over again. *England has changed*—and besides, I've no one there—no brothers or sisters. My home is here, Anil—in these hills, among these trees. (75–76; emphasis mine)

The projected alteration, understandably, of sociocultural space in England is not imaginary but derives from the author-persona's first-hand knowledge that transmutes into Miss Mackenzie's apprehension. With this knowledge of change, the absence of 'emotional space' is obliquely signalled. The next chapter will state how Bond's negligence of 'emotional space' in Dehra induced traumatic experiences outside India.

Journey to the Centre of the Self

'The journey as a trope for growth, learning, the unfolding of personal or collective experience, and for life itself,' writes Ashis Nandy, 'has been a favourite of philosophers, scholars and mystics in South Asia for centuries' (2001, 8). The idea of my subtitle is taken from the third chapter of Nandy's book. Let me explain why. In *The Room*, a 16-year-old-boy is the protagonist. The novelist asks in his 1993 introduction to *The Room on the Roof and Vagrants in the Valley: Two Novels of Adolescence*: 'Who was he, and where did he come from? Was he an Indian or an Anglo-Indian or an English boy born in India?' (vii). He immediately adds:

> I have since answered these questions for myself, certain that I am as Indian as the dust of the plains or the grass of a mountain meadow; but as a young man I had no such certainties, and to some extent Rusty represents the dilemma I faced. (ibid.)

The authorial identity has to overcome this initial quandary before he can sense his 'Indian' self. In the course of action, when Rusty realises the shortcomings of his guardian's narrow horizon, he decentres himself from it, and connects with the wider secularised cultural currents—albeit Dehra's bazaar. The knowledge of Rusty's bazaar visit compels his guardian to warn: 'The point is, I have told you never to visit the bazaar. You belong here, to this house, this road, these people. Don't go where you don't belong' (2010, 20). Just as Dehra's Anglo-Indianness should not be confused with the generalised idea of Anglo-Indianness, Bond's inclination should not be reviewed as a prototype of Anglo-Indian expression. Rusty's approach might not necessarily have been the same as other mixed-blood adolescents in India, but such allowance is necessitated in the narrative to denote Rusty's trajectory from ambivalence to openness.

One of the primary concerns of the text, I argue, lies in Rusty's *bodh*, and this *bodh* exists outside the 'ifs' and 'thens' of racial amalgamation. It is also to be noted that the racial superiority and social snobbery that Mr Harrison, rusty's guardian, boasts of compel him to look down upon the other Indians and treat them negatively, which in turn distances him socially, culturally and even psychologically from the other Indian natives. Mr Harrison's class-consciousness refers back to the colonial past. As Gist and Wright have examined in *Marginality and Identity*:

> It [Anglo-Indian Community] is marginal socially because it is not extensively integrated into the organized social fabric of the larger society. It is marginal culturally because the basic culture of the Community—religion, family organization, language, styles of life—separates Anglo-Indians from the majority of other Indians. It is marginal psychologically because the attitudes and images, often reflecting social and cultural differences, one such as to create and maintain social distances between the Anglo-Indians and others. Taken together these attributes—social, cultural, psychological—represent barriers which have had the effect of limiting or obstructing social interaction and cultural exchange between the people of the sub-continent. (151)

Bond's upbringing and development of identity in secular space, in fact, help Rusty in his act of distancing himself from the Anglo-Indian ghetto of Dehra. The authorial urge to channelise his strained adolescence into something desirable is recognisable in his fictional self too. His adolescent memories, which went through discontents, paint a convincing alter-life in fiction. Rusty is very much Ruskin Bond, more than mere fictional representation, more than a fellow Anglo-Indian boy. Therefore, more often than not, he is given expression to fortify the author's unfulfilled wish. Thus Rusty's voyage in *The Room* in a way envisages Bond's personal independence in Dehra after his return from Britain. It is quite striking in the way in which the author undergoes an emancipating experience by directing his hero to follow his individual will.

Rusty has never lived, the novelist's literary output suggests, outside India. We notice that Rusty's desire to secularise himself by challenging his guardian's English orthodoxy lies in his deliberate pursuit of personal space. In *The Room*, it seems, Bond the novelist is creating Rusty out of his own inadequacies. Rusty the hero is an ardent learner of life; he likes to dream and live. 'What does freedom mean to an "Anglo-Indian"'? the novel asks. The text also proposes a possibility through which Rusty's choice to live with other Indians is established, and the proposal, if we address it so, seems convincing. Rusty's objection is not against the communal differences but against his community's illusions and biases that blind one's reasoning and individuation. His choice to leave his guardian's sphere—a prejudiced European order—can, therefore, be seen as an act of decolonising the mind. It further enables the boy of mixed-descent to see beyond his hybrid origin so as to find his root in wider terrain. Mr Harrison's world view only hyphenates Rusty's domicile in India, complicating his sense of belonging in his motherland. In *Domicile and Diaspora* (2005) Alison Blunt mentions that instead of identifying their Indian compatriots as 'kinsmen', many Anglo-Indians tended to consider their Indian compatriots primarily as servants: 'Just as British imperial domesticity reproduced "empires in the home", Anglo-Indian relations with their Indian servants underpinned wider processes of differentiation both within and beyond the domestic sphere' (56). On this ground, we can assume Mr Harrison's perception of the rest of the Indians outside his community. The narrative, reasonably, never relies on the propagandist viewpoint of Mr Harrison. No glorification of Englishness is adverted here. No jibe is made against the rituals of the 'natives'. Other than the illusioned Mr Harrison, no stereotypical character representation is put forward to highlight imperial hangover. If there are instances of irrationality and emotive outbursts among Somi and his friends, these are very Indian or what an Indian imagination encompasses. Rusty's preference to roam around with his new (and only) friends denotes his inclination to associate with wider cultural variances and not to limit himself into any political positioning. It is also to be noted that even if Ruskin Bond is Anglo-Indian by birth and brought up in an Anglo-Indian household, none of his works is set outside the consciousness of what we mean by 'Indian'. By this, I mean, rather than identifying merely with communal existence (which can also be Indian), it is more of identifying himself with everything Indian. Such liberating insight is possible only when one becomes a true 'insider'. Rusty's individuality thus grows out of this realisation. If there is a single display of coloniser's supremacy from Mr Harrison, it is meant only to be challenged. If there is any sarcasm meted out by the novelist, it is directed towards Mr Harrison's 'English' attitude.

Despite such a vast scope, there are perhaps three primary reasons why Bond's debut venture in 1956 failed to achieve immediate attention abroad. First, Bond was considered to be an outsider, a mixed-blood who is in pursuit of 'home' in Britain. Further, when the novel was published, he had already left England, never to return. Second, although it was an original story, it failed to match the general English taste. Since Britain had already read Rumer Godden, M.M. Kaye, John Masters, Paul Scott and some others by the mid-1950s, it was not difficult to label a sentimental work about India as a nostalgic tenor of the Raj experience. Finally and perhaps most significantly, the initial critical neglect of *The Room*, especially in the Indian subcontinent, despite the praises in some of the frontline dailies and magazines, was because young-adult literature as a genre was yet to be recognised.

The literary career of Ruskin Bond is best understood through reading his memoirs, where his merits on narrative ease and authorial reticence are simultaneously balanced. *Scenes from a Writer's Life* (1997) is one such example that allows readers to see the otherwise ordinary side of 'Dehra'—a living physicality providing him confidence to conjoin with its spirit. The liberating sense Dehra is endowed with results from this reliance. In the following chapter, I shall study the reasons behind Bond's departure from the place of origin to a mythically ideal land. Writing the journal also serves the act of retreading his personal self, thereby reappraising his present identity. To make his point viable, he has already made semi-autobiographical 'Rusty'—which, when pronounced, gives similar auditory sensation as 'Ruskin'—and put him almost in similar situations which Bond the novelist has already experienced.

As is the case of many other mixed-blood people, Ruskin Bond, advertently or inadvertently, neglects the environment in India—where he has grown up—before he comes to realise that Britain is really an imaginary homeland. Bond's expatriation to Britain is a rollercoaster ride into his otherwise ordinary life. The sojourn to his detriment, therefore, turns out to be an all-new experience. In fact, what this sojourn does to Bond, Dehra's bazaar does almost the same to Rusty. An eye-opener, Rusty's participation in *chaat*-shop *adda* (a carefree and informal conversation among a group in India) comes not merely as an experience to see the 'real' India but to see the life of his country, which he is a part of:

> The shop was crowded; but so thick was the screen of smoke and steam, that it was only the murmur of conversation which made known the

> presence of many people. A plate made of banana leaves was thrust into Rusty's hands, and two fried cakes suddenly appeared in it.
>
> 'Eat!' said Somi, pressing the novice down until they were both on the floor, their backs to the wall.
>
> 'They are tikkees,' explained Somi, 'tell me if you like them.'
>
> Rusty tasted a bit. It was hot. He waited a minute, then tasted another bit. It was still hot but in a different way; now it was lively, interesting; it had a different taste to anything he had eaten before. Suspicious but inquisitive, he finished the tikkee and waited to see if anything would happen. (Bond 2010, 15–16)

In my understanding of Bond's third novel, *A Flight of Pigeons* (originally appeared in the 1970s) suggests two aspects that often interweave with each other but none mellows the other. First, the novelist refrains from prioritising the 1857 Revolt, often emotionally labelled as India's First War of Independence, as his key focus. We notice how Shahjahanpur, where the novel is set, is agitated with the revolt of the *sepoys* against the ruling British, but we are also told about the damage done by the mutineers to the *angrez*. Instead of being authoritative, Bond lets his readers be opinionated. The second aspect, where I specifically focus, is a humane tale of mutual respect and affection, wherein undoing stereotypical notions, a convincing effort is invested to delineate how a mixed-blood (Eurasian) woman during the mid-19th century associates herself with other Indian natives. Bond seems to uphold how human goodness rises above religion, class and race. We also learn how the 'natives' of the town help Mariam and her family in difficult hours. Clearly, Bond's approach here seems to uphold an anti-stereotypical stance to stress that it is partially true that Anglo-Indian (erstwhile Eurasian) women were prejudiced against Indian 'natives'. In fact, the tendency among the mixed-blood people to accept one culture while renouncing the other has been a matter of critical inquiry. Alison Blunt in *Domicile and Diaspora* comments that the community preferred the Western culture more often due to the predominance of the British Raj:

> Unlike other Christians in India, the European ancestry of Anglo-Indians—reflected by cultural markers such as language, dress and eating habits—continued to shape a distinctive community identity that was bound to Europe, and particularly Britain, as home.
>
> Although Anglo-Indians were of a lower social status and poorer than the British elite in India, everyday life in an Anglo-Indian home was much closer to British than Indian domesticity. Middle-class Anglo-Indian women read many of the same household guides as British memsahibs, and, as already noted, employed Indian servants to cook and clean. Meals in both British and Anglo-Indian homes combined a distinctive mixture of western and Indian food, and were eaten with cutlery rather than by hand, and sitting at a table rather than on the floor. (2005, 53)

Like the British *memsahibs*, Anglo-Indian women were directly responsible for the management of their servants in particular and of their household in general. Although they often conversed with them in Hindi, class superiority still prevailed. Mariam's openness to overcome this class discretion is rare but not inconceivable. Despite the fact that Mariam is born and brought up in India she is thought to be a *firangan* precisely due to her *métis* birth. No wonder, as we will see later in Muslim households, they are mocked as 'enchantress' because of their blue eyes and fair hair. It is at this point that Mariam's immaculate knowledge of Muslim customs earns her respect. The narrative focus on depicting Mariam's acceptance among other Indians also promises a liberal attitude that the novelist desires to establish.

A Handful of Nuts (1996), a fusion of autobiography, fiction and history, is a work through which the author-persona revisits his early youth to recast his authorial self in Indian life so that a true reflection of evolved identity is perceived. It is a tale of kinship with Dehra's everydayness and how this affinity shapes him as a human being. In other words, by recalling his youthful past, Bond puts himself outside the binary of pre-colonial/postcolonial framework to chisel his *desi* statuesque. In a way, the novel is a tribute to his favourite town which, far from being a mere setting, chants the shared affinity of the author. This novel, therefore, materialises how the author sees the town. Dehra in the novel is not commented on but alive through familiarity. Besides challenging easy assumptions about the formation of identity of postcolonial subjects, including of all those who have taken Kipling, for instance, to be on the imperial side, *A Handful of Nuts* seeks to engage both present and past and explores the author-narrator's newly evolved identity in independent India.

In this narrative, again, Dehra is caught in the mid-1950s—an important phase when the authorial identity has returned after a period of estrangement. Ruskin Bond went to Britain when he was 17 and returned to India when he was 21. The novel is entrusted with the youthful days of the 21st-year of the anonymous protagonist, visibly the fictional self of the novelist, who struggles to live through hardship. A considerable part of the narrative revolves around Rusty's 21st birthday preparation, celebration, and its aftermath. Despite the narrative wandering at different nooks of life, it is emotionally coherent. However, written as late as in the 1990s by a mature Bond, the apparent contestation of East/West binary is readily overlooked, and is replaced by a familiar space in which the authorial self unhesitatingly unravels himself.

Does Dehradun exist in Indian writing in English so prominently outside Bond's world? The question does not perhaps need an answer. It is not the first time that an Indian English writer fictionalises India from abroad; Raja Rao did it while writing *Kanthapura* (1938), R.K. Narayan did it in case of *The Guide* (1958) during his three months stay in Berkeley. Interestingly, all three novels have strong settings and reasonably good characterisation. But, where Dehra stands apart is that the novelist does not write fiction on it, but allows Dehra-ness to permeate into fiction. If Bond's writing is a true reservoir of Indian life on one side, the occasional references to English education and culture on the other verifies a mixed-cultural assonance, which is common amidst post-independent subcontinent set-ups. Dehra's Larry Gomes's felicity in performing old English classics and recent

Bollywood hits in *A Handful of Nuts* denotes that colonial legacy is not always negative. In *The Twice Born Fiction* (2001), Meenakshi Mukherjee substantiates:

> In the complex fabric of contemporary Indian civilisation, the two most easily discerned strands are the indigenous Indian traditions and the imported European conceptions. Almost every educated Indian today is the product of the conflicts and reconciliations of two cultures, although the consciousness of this tension varies from individual to individual. What is generally true of the educated Indian is especially true of the Indian writer, because a writer is concerned with the springs of human action and with the motivation behind human behaviour. [. . .] At the present point of Indian history, a writer's analysis of his self necessarily involves the evaluation of his own attitude towards these two aspects of his being—one inherited from birth, the other imbibed through education. (69)

Mukherjee adds that cultural coalescing—be it an infringement or 'synthesis'—has been a critical implication for the 'Indian novelist who writes in English' (69). *A Handful of Nuts* hardly addresses the age-old dichotomy on the 'meeting' between the East and the West, yet the East-West motif is implicitly stepped in to demonstrate the elasticity of cultural blending.

In Chapter 3, I tackle how Rusty's individual temperament is complicated by his communal existence. My engagement to follow Rusty's desire to see beyond his ghettoised positioning may be questioned from another (and perhaps numerous other) standpoint(s). But, to me, this seems more relevant to this study. In Chapter 4, I contend that Bond's interpretation of Ruth's story, far from receding to a jejune retelling, reviews India's tolerant attitude towards caste, class, religion and race. Therefore Mariam, unlike the European women of Shahjahanpur, who compartmentalise themselves from other Indians out of class superiority and racial hierarchy, is rather invited to socialise with them. Chapter 5 is preoccupied with a slightly older Rusty's eagerness to 'see' India. With his new state of consciousness, attained through self-questioning, the hero's view of Dehra finds a renewed perception. To extend this argument, I partially rely on Jiddu Krishnamurti's philosophical understanding of human conditions. In one of his talks, later anthologised in *On Nature and the Environment* (2006), Krishnamurti examines:

> There is no foundation for true thinking unless we know ourselves. Without knowing myself, I have no foundation for thought—I can only live in a state of contradiction, as most of us do. [. . .] To understand oneself is to understand one's relationship with things, people, and ideas. (7)

The evolution of the authorial identity from being in a position preoccupied with negotiating his racial identification to constantly viewing India in a secularised format enlightens Ruskin Bond's Indian consciousness (which is entwined with modernity) and helps him invest in a recognisable outlook. It is with this idea of ceaseless development that Bond advances towards Rusty-stories, while the readers, instead of being well aware of the boy's racial complexity, seem to consider him nothing but an Indian. In this exploration, one can observe a direct connection between his subject and location, because Bond's writing is directly inspired by Indian settings and experiences. With this, Dehra in Rusty's case and Shahjahanpur in Mariam's energise the central figures' rebellious sentiment to exercise the act of developing awareness. This is how the intimacy of the author-narrator with his setting that I bring out in Chapter 5 translates into an embodied meditation of *desh*.

Ruskin Bond's literary output begins with angst and continues to be a ceaseless pursuit for self-making. From this ground, the inception of a semi-autobiographical self can be rationalised. Of course, Bond's abiding concern for subjectivity makes his oeuvre immediate and distinctive. But, this assumption is fairly impossible without the exchange between his public and private selves. The rapport between the fictional identity and the lived-one, therefore, becomes integral to the premise on which Bond's writing is formulated. To read his works is, in turn, to read the individual hidden behind them. In the discussion that follows, I shall contextualise Bond's authorial 'self' before examining the fictional route(s) that he takes.

Notes

1. Mussoorie and Landour are twin towns located in the foothills of the Himalayas at an altitude of some 7,000 feet. In Mussoorie, Ruskin Bond stayed in the Maplewood Lodge for more than a decade before he permanently moved up to Ivy Cottage, Landour, with his extended family in 1981.
2. Bond's works convey an inside-Indian perspective, which comes from his innate understating of his roots. For a detailed analysis, see the following chapters.
3. 'Anglo-Indian' is a complicated term. Initially, the expression 'Anglo-Indian' referred to the Englishmen living in India, whereas the term 'Eurasian' was employed to mean mixed-blood people. Muthiah and MacLure write: 'It was in the 1911 census that the government of Lord Hardinge officially termed those of mixed-blood, children born of European fathers and Indian mothers and children born of their offspring, as "Anglo-India"' (2003, 1). For more, see *The Anglo-Indians: A 500-Year History* by S. Muthiah and Harry MacLure.
4. The aesthetic of Bond's writing deepens through his close intimacy with Nature. In *When Darkness Falls and Other Stories* (2001), he informs: 'My inspiration, or subject matter if you like, has always come from my Indian background and experience—my relationship to people, the landscape, the atmosphere' (ibid., ix).
5. The interview was held on 6 April 2016 at Ruskin Bond's residence in Landour.

Bibliography

Alter, Stephen. 2008. *Neglected Lives*. New Delhi: Penguin.

Anthony, Frank. 1969. *Britain's Betrayal in India: The Story of the Anglo-Indian Community*. New Delhi: Allied Publishers.

Blunt, Alison. 2005. *Domicile and Diaspora: Anglo-Indian Women and the Spatial Politics of Home*. Oxford: Blackwell Publishing.

Bond, Ruskin. 1988. 'The Man Who Was Kipling', *The Night Train at Deoli and Other Stories*. New Delhi: Penguin, 31–33.

———. 1988. *The Night Train at Deoli and Other Stories*. New Delhi: Penguin.

———. 1992. 'Kipling's Simla', *Strange Men Strange Places*. New Delhi: Rupa, 85–90.

———. 1993. *The Room on the Roof and Vagrants in the Valley: Two Novels of Adolescence*. New Delhi: Penguin.

———. 2001. *When Darkness Falls and Other Stories*. Haryana: Penguin.

———. 2010. 'The Room on the Roof', *Classic Ruskin Bond Vol. 1: The Novels*. New Delhi: Penguin, 1–114.

———. 2012. 'Introduction', *Just So Stories*. By Rudyard Kipling. New Delhi: Rupa, vii–x.

———. 2012. 'Scenes from a Writer's Life', *Classic Ruskin Bond Vol. 2: The Memoirs*. New Delhi: Penguin, 253–404.

———. 2015. *A Book of Simple Living: Brief Notes from the Hills*. New Delhi: Speaking Tiger.

———. 2017. *Lone Fox Dancing: My Autobiography*. New Delhi: Speaking Tiger.

Caplan, Lionel. 2001. *Children of Colonialism: Anglo-Indians in a Postcolonial World*. Oxford: Berg.

Chaudhuri, Amit. 2018. *The Origins of Dislike*. New Delhi: Oxford University Press.

Gist, Noel Pitts and Roy Dean Wright. 1973. *Marginality and Identity: Anglo-Indians as a Racially-Mixed Minority in India*. Leiden: E.J. Brill.

Harris, Jonathan Gil. 2015. *The First Firangis*. New Delhi: Aleph.

James, Sheila Pais. 2003. 'The Anglo-Indians: Aspirations for Whiteness and the Dilemma of Identity', *Counterpoints*. Web. 12 December 2016, 50–60.

Khorana, Meena G. 2003. *The Life and Works of Ruskin Bond*. Westport, CT: Praeger.

Kipling, Rudyard. 2009. *Selected Poems (Everyman Classics)*. Gurgaon: Hachette India, 27–31.

Krishnamurthy, J. 2006. *On Nature and the Environment*. New Delhi: Penguin.

Lahiri-Dutt, Kuntala. 2011. 'Anglo-Indians as Part of the Indian Diaspora: Making a Home in Australia'. *South Asia Masala*. 11 May. Available at: http://asiapacific.anu.edu.au/blogs/southasiamasala/2011/05/11/feature-article-anglo-indians-as-part-of-the-indian-diaspora-making-a-home-in-australia/ (accessed on 13 May 2015).

Masters, John. 1983. *Bhowani Junction*. London: Sphere Books.

Melwani, Murli Das. 1995. 'The Gentle Voice of Indo-Anglian Literature', *The Creative Contours of Ruskin Bond: An Anthology of Critical Writings*. Ed. Prabhat K. Singh. New Delhi: Pencraft Publications, 41–45.

Moore, Gloria J. 1996. 'A Brief History of the Anglo-Indians.' *IJAIS*. Web. 12 December 2016, 50–58.

Mukherjee, Meenakshi. 2001. *The Twice Born Fiction: Themes and Techniques of the Indian Novel in English*. New Delhi: Pencraft.

Muthiah, S. and Harry MacLure. 2013. *The Anglo-Indians: A 500-Year History*. New Delhi: Niyogi Books.

Nandy, Ashis. 2001. *An Ambiguous Journey to the City*. New Delhi: Oxford University Press.

Peppin, Bryan. 2012. *Black and White: The "Anglo-Indian" Identity in Recent English Fiction*. Central Milton Keynes, UK: Author House. Kindle.

Renan, Ernest. 1990. 'What Is a Nation'. In *Nation and Narration*, edited by Homi K. Bhabha. London: Routledge, 8–22.

Sealy, Irwin Allan. 1988. *The Trotter Nama*. New York: Knopf.

———. 2008. *The Constitution of India*. Delhi: Universal Law Publishing.

2

Desh-Videsh

Scenes as Dialectics of Homecoming

At the end of the First World War, the conditions of Anglo-Indians in India started to deteriorate socially and economically due to some national schemes favouring 'Indian' natives, especially after their demarcation as the 'statutory natives of India' by the British. As a result, the Anglo-Indians tended to consider themselves as 'part of an imperial diaspora in British India' (Blunt 2005, 2). Once the British left India, the Anglo-Indians sensed a loss of familial support and found themselves in a condition that unfailingly induced in them a feeling of uprootedness in India—a place where they had been born and brought up. They even considered the changed sociopolitical condition as a loss of right to stay in India. The contemporary cultural-historical cosmos, amidst the sentiment of a free sovereign country, worked somewhat contrarily for them. Indian independence, erratically but emphatically, put them in a zone, which, to borrow from Homi Bhabha, can be explained as an awkward situation that 'captures something of the estranging sense of the relocation of the home and the world in an unhallowed place' (Bhabha 2015, 141). The sense of being 'unhomed', Bhabha observed, complicated its recipient's sense of belonging by pushing him back to a nebulous state and making life feel 'as if in parenthesis'. The Anglo-Indians' credo that 'home is only abroad'—a space yet to be seen—advocates their sense of 'unhomeliness' in India. Their 'unhomed' positioning, in fact, emanated from their psychological and sociocultural displacement in India by the British colonial policy on the one hand, and spurious nationalism on the other. This is how, as Bhabha maintains, '[t]he unhomely moment relates the traumatic ambivalences of a personal, psychic history to the wider disjunctions of political existence' (144) reinforcing one's estrangement from his root. It is, however, interesting to note that despite the Anglo-Indians' inclination to European culture, the idea that India was always in their thoughts and activities gave them certitude.

As the title suggests, the present chapter examines the historical context in order to delve into the core of Bond's sojourn to Britain, the 'fatherland' of British/European residents in their colonial imagination, and his subsequent return to India. Writing in 1926, amidst nationalist tensions and the Anglo-Indians' imagination of idolising Britain as their true home, Herbert Stark envisaged what could have been the voice of the community: 'If England is the land of our fathers, India is the land of our mothers. If to us England is a hallowed memory, India is a living verity. If England is the land of our pilgrimage, India is the land of our homes' (131). But, behind this sentiment lurked a lucrative choice for economic betterment abroad. This came from, what Stark feared, a dubiousness about their prospects within India with the establishment of a new Indian government. The fear of an uncertain future led them to doubt their status as citizens of the country in post-independent India.

Ruskin Bond's moving away from the place of his birth to Britain, however, is not only the result of an Anglo-Indian complex existential angst but also the expression of something with multifarious rationale about which I shall discuss. Written in a deeply personal tone, *Scenes from a Writer's Life* (1997) (henceforth *Scenes*) abounds in Bond's philosophical rigour, reflecting both his literary journey as well as his personal one. The relevance of the journal in this discussion is important not merely because the book reviews the first 21 years of the author's life—the delicate, emotional and formative years of hardship, failure and hope—but because it produces some indelible insights necessary to understand the Bondian oeuvre. Seen alternatively, *Scenes* upholds a sensitive youth's journey to maturity, and in turn, reproduces some glimpses into the shaping of authorial identity. In

1997, Penguin India's decision to publish the memoir to mark India's 50th anniversary of independence is greatly significant as a kind of implication to commemorate the national self.

Sojourn to Britain: Oscillation in 'Adopted Home'

The year 1947 marked the independence of India as a free sovereign nation on the one hand, and on the other, it intensified the dilemma of the Anglo-Indian community. Although the Anglo-Indian exodus took place throughout the colonial period, post-1947 gave birth to, what Lionel Caplan proposes, 'a culture of emigration' (2015, 26) in the history of the community's existence. The sudden dwindling of the Anglo-Indian population significantly affected the lives of those who stayed back; this trend of emigration that largely spread out wards from the artisan class created havoc in their psyche. They had to negotiate myriads of complications—social and cultural marginalisation amidst economic difficulties made them uneasy. Till this juncture Anglo-Indians had kept a relatively low profile; they were neither a professionally skilled, highly educated urban milieu, nor were they uneducated and unskilled. Though they were relatively devoted to the Western (especially British) culture and their inclination towards Indianisation was majorly overlooked, no judicious argument can be made (except in some exceptional cases) disfavouring their Indian way of living. The idea that they were primarily 'Europeans' was profoundly infused into their consciousness. This forced them to believe that they were different from 'Indians'. That is to say, the ruling British were successful in fostering their politicised identity. Their preference, consequently, towards accepting British culture, sidelining their Indian roots, inculcated in them a sense that it was only abroad (mainly Britain or any other European country) that their true roots could be found. In one of his articles, Caplan says,

> Thus, despite persistent British denials of kinship with Anglo-Indians, a variety of day-to-day circumstances and practices reinforced Eurasian convictions in their exclusive European blood and culture,

> and contributed to the widespread belief that Anglo-Indians belonged to a society other than their own and to a place other than India. (2015, 31)

In fact, their decision to go abroad emerged out of their insistence on seeing themselves as religiously, culturally and morally Europeans, and, more importantly, out of the idyllic notion that life in the West could only be a panacea for security, social and economic stability. Caplan notes that in 1942, the Anglo-Indian Association 'urged the colonial authorities to allow Anglo-Indians the opportunity to emigrate to any part of the British Empire' (2001, 133) assuming that the new regime in India might not entertain economic privileges and that Britain would offer better working opportunities. It was like choosing the seemingly easier alternative based on the assumption that they had no fortune in India unless they were well qualified or affluent.

With the Indian constitutional inclusion of the community in 1951 yet to happen, those who stayed back, according to some scholars in this field, seriously doubted their fortune in this country; the sense of alienation, generated both from hybrid identity and nationalist idiom, led them to leave their birthplace. Commenting on the vexation in the post-independent scenario, Caplan assesses:

> Anglo-Indians have gradually lost their protected status they enjoyed in certain occupied niches, and have had to survive in an unsteady economic climate, increasingly subject to global influences which have, if anything, adversely affected those least educated and skilled. Without the protection afforded to 'scheduled castes' or 'back-ward classes'—who comprise the bulk of the disadvantaged in the contemporary Indian society—the Anglo-Indian poor feel themselves to be suffering disproportionately. At the same time, the colonial ceiling which confined Anglo-Indians within certain work spaces lifted with the withdrawal of the British . . . . (2003, 16)

Besides the fact that their 'history of support for the raj' (Caplan 2001, 33) might work against their interest in post-independent India, they were worried because of the developing competitive market from the early decades of the 20th century; their job market was challenged by educated Indian middle class.

In the section titled 'Dehradun—Winter of '45' of his book *A Town Called Dehra* (2008), Ruskin Bond briefly highlights the crises of Dehradun's domiciled Europeans and the further consequences of the crises. The young, unmarried Anglo-Indian girls of Dehra would occasionally be involved in affairs with British or American soldiers who roistered in town during the Second World War; such affairs would often end up in marriages, whisking the girls away like Doreen from India. It is to be underlined that '[f]or many Anglo-Indians and "poor whites", assisted passages to England were the order of the day' (Bond 2008, 24). Apart from qualifying himself as a 'poor white', the memoirist maintains that the time saw even the worst of the segregation. In this regard he narrates the misery and hardship of homeless Mrs Deeds and her 17-year-old son (Howard), who, having none to ask for help, had to live in a small room in the back of Green's Hotel (where Bond's mother used to work as a manager) before they moved out under compulsion. Having failed to pay the hotel dues, they spent many days on the railway platform. In the text, they were defined as 'the flotsam of Empire, jettisoned by the very people who had brought them into existence' (25–26). Mrs Deeds possibly belonged to the social order that had neither professional skills for sustenance in India nor financial aids to immediately afford a 'better' future overseas. Miss Kellner, another unfortunate, was beaten and raped by a gang of three or four men, thereby restricting her life to a wheelchair. Such 'paralysed' life along with vulnerability and wretchedness of the poor-whites was deeply registered in Ruskin Bond's psyche, and this presumably made him aware that the contemporary sociopolitical situation in India somewhat went against the poor-whites. The colonial consequences and post-War aftermath with an apprehension of the apathy of the new government made these poor-whites shaky and disorganised. Bond's scrutinisation of the community building upon the idea of human flotsam thus is not without base and ensures trauma of displacement. Imagining Britain as a possible alternative, even if one would end up at a working-class district, in order to escape from a baffling sphere seemed easier. It is to be remembered that written in the 1990s, the reportage given in *Scenes* is not without Bond's first-hand experiences of the working-class areas of Britain.

Bond's grandmother Ellen Clerk, who died on the eve of Indian Independence, was a concerned grandparent. Miss Kellner, her tenant, who expressed to Bond her wish to leave India about a year before, died in 1951, giving him forewarning that the rest of Dehradun's domiciled Europeans would soon be effaced either by natural demise or by overseas emigration. Since Bond was the sole remaining youth in their locality, he rationalised that the time was not far away to encounter reality:

> I have always enjoyed the company of older people because they have interesting stories and experiences to relate—provided, of course, they do not repeat themselves to the point of boredom. Granny, oddly enough, had never been one for reminiscence, but Miss Kellner had often overburdened herself to me [. . .]. (2012, 334)

This void in turn initiated camaraderie with local 'Indians', whom he had left behind at Bishop Cotton School (Shimla) and with Azhar (Bond calls him Omar in an autobiographical story 'The Playing Fields of Simla'): 'There was Ranbir and his super sister Raj; there was Bhim, already making little business deals; and there were other families in the mohalla, such as the Lals (who became the Kapoors in *The Room on the Roof*) and the Sikh boys—Haripal, Dipi, Somi and Chotu . . .' (2012, 335). Among them, Bond became close to Somi, who gave him a curious look at their first meeting, which actually grew out of admiration and surprise that a 17-year-old boy has published a story in *The Illustrated Weekly of India*, a weekly Indian magazine, and also because of an odd resemblance with the Victorian author John Ruskin, whose essay in the syllabus troubled Somi immensely. Bond's sympathetic reply that he, too, failed to understand anything of the particular essay pleased Somi, and this set the foundation of their bonding. The time he spent with Somi was both thrilling and fulfilling, and this would reflect in his writing too. Such affinity with Somi also gave Ruskin Bond a sense of faith that even though he had lost his Anglo-Indian relatives one after another, everything was not lost yet. Thus one day, inspired by common hopes and dreams, Bond dedicates a short poem to Somi: 'Hold on to your dreams,/Do not let them die./We are lame without them—/Birds that cannot fly' (2008, 336). This revitalising phase of life is, however, halted as he somewhat agrees 'to go to England to live for some time with my [his] Aunt Emily' (336). The decision, no less political on his part, is taken to fulfil his dream of becoming a 'published' author, and seemingly to get closer to the literary heroes he has read. Since there is better scope for literary exposure in Britain as compared to the subcontinent, he decides to move away despite a strong desire to come back. Just before his lonely sojourn to Britain, on being asked by Haripal, Somi's elder brother and one of his friends, whether he really wanted to go to England, Bond replies: 'For the career, yes; otherwise, no. I've got used to this place' (338). The other day, when Bond meets Haripal's mother for the first time, he is touched by her acceptance and friendliness: 'You must come to our house whenever you like, it is yours. And, when you are not very busy you can teach Chotu [the youngest brother of Haripal] English; he is very lazy and always fails in his tests' (341). It was, therefore, a period of vacillation—on the one hand, he starts understanding India keenly; on the other, he is partially fascinated by literary England that could drive him for the rest of his life. In a self-reflexive tone, he summarises the angst that is the voice of many Anglo-Indians staying/leaving India at that point of time:

> In a rushing, materialistic world of doers I shall most likely be a failure, and I'll be sorry for ever having given up this life. I can write here—anywhere—but it is the desire for recognition and applause that lures me away. I tell myself that fame is not greatness, and that if I remain as I am long enough I shall soon grow accustomed to obscurity. At least I shall retain my individuality, and in art that is most important.

> In the west I shall start following this trend and that, fashions and styles and topicality. I shall probably emerge a hack, one of thousands.
>
> I can still write if I remain here, even though few will read my work; and there, who knows, nobody might read me. (2008, 359–60)

His biographical determination of 'I do not want to go, but I must' is later altered in his fictional corpus as 'I may go, but why shall I go?', or 'why shall I compromise my personal touch with India for a materialistic purpose?' Whatsoever the dilemma was, Bond was certain about his return even before he had set out, something he has shared with me in a personal interview.[1]

Elsewhere in *Scenes*, Bond defends Aubrey by arguing that his father's insistence on settling abroad does not determine the fact that he was an advocate of the empire because his decision was based on a practical purpose of gaining a livelihood. Bond's intimacy with his father can be assumed at how he, always taking his father's side, could freely express his disagreement with his mother. Even amidst his hectic military duties as an RAF (The Royal Air Force) appointee during the War (Second World War) days, Aubrey Bond, like a concerned father, would keep in touch with his elder son through letters and advise him on numerous aspects of life. Bond's understanding that his parents were mismatched to each other came a little later. Aubrey's sensibility towards life, which did pass on to his son, differed completely from Edith's outlook. His mother, in her early-twenties-motherhood, was brimming with youthful vigour and supposedly preferred sensuousness to her husband's middle-aged sensibility. The union of Aubrey and Edith was not the marriage of minds, and therefore conjugal clash was imminent. Edith's celebratory youth, Bond later recognises, was against Aubrey's aesthetic calmness; his mother's 'fun-loving' efflorescence was, not unsurprisingly, in disagreement with the father's reasonableness. And this led her to get involved with a Punjabi businessman, Mr Harbans Lal (Hari), who with his flamboyant nature impressed Edith's youthful exuberance. The daily sense of discomfort at his stepfather's house affected his teenage self.

Hari was neither cruel nor unkind to him; but his youth and *joie de vivre* made him someone who, the memoirist writes, 'hadn't the sensitivity to make a go of being a "father"' (2008, 291).

When Ruskin Bond was (presumably) eight, his parents separated; when he was only ten, Aubrey Bond passed away. His father's sudden demise not only truncated a loving relationship but also pushed Bond into utter confusion—should he now stay with his grandmother (from his father's side) in Calcutta, or with his mother, or simply go to an orphanage? The loss was irreparable for this 10-year-old child, and Bond found none to share his feelings with until he would fictionalise some of those moments years later. Bond expresses to Ganesh Saili: 'As there was no evidence of my father's death, it was, for me, not a death but a vanishing, and to this day, I subconsciously expect him to turn up (as he indeed often did, when I most needed him) and deliver me from bad situations' (Saili 2004, 38). Aubrey Bond's influence on his son is so impressive that even Diana Athill, Bond's editor, cannot but express: 'Although Ruskin and his father were able to share only a short part of life, that part was composed of by far the most formative... Yes! He made Ruskin a writer, and that is Ruskin's centre' (46). Bond accepted his father's demise much later when he visited the latter's grave at the Bhowanipore War Cemetery (Kolkata) with Maya Banerjee: 'It was only in the winter of 2001, at the age of sixty-seven, that he was able to bring himself to believe that his father was gone [. . .]' (38). The deprivation of maternal care, which he really missed at his father's absence and which was the only reliable face outside his friend circle at school, irked the youth. His restlessness was further deepened due to his mother's remarriage, which he particularly resented:

> My mother and Mr. Hari went out almost every night. The old Ford convertible would bring them back at two or three in the morning. My insecurity was such that I would often wonder how I would cope if they had a fatal accident coming home, or if some avenging tigress got her own back in the jungle. Would I have to look after my sister, baby brother and two half-bothers? And where would the money come from? (2008, 297)

Their reckless lifestyle—something which Bond disliked—is naturally not literalised in any of his works. His step father's motor-garage business was gradually declining; and to Bond's dismay, he was eventually bankrupt. It is not unexpected that considering Mr Harbans Lal's declining business and their imminent economic misery, Edith Clerke made the practical choice of sending her oldest son to her elder sister who had already settled in the Channel Islands. At this point, he, being the eldest child of the family, considered himself a burden—a fact that can be seen in his act of leaving home and living on railway platforms and park benches during a quarrel with his mother. His consequent decision to return and stay in a *barsati* (literally, the rooftop) till he was able to manage on his own reflects pride, self-respect and the ambition of self-establishment. The search for a room of one's own was inevitable both for personal and artistic vocation. The discomfort with his mother and stepfather and the suppressed desire to become a published author worked together to make his voyage possible. It will, therefore, be an over simplification to see Ruskin Bond's sojourn to England primarily as validation for possible recognition as a published writer. Had he not been there, he would perhaps have not realised his sentiment for and tie with India as passionately as he felt immediately afterwards. Therefore, his journey, as says Meena Khorana, 'can be seen as the quest of an archetypal hero whose courage and determination would enable him to resolve his identity crisis and to pursue his ambition of becoming a published author' (2003, 25).

Bond's unease in family space, after finishing his Senior Cambridge from Bishop Cotton School (Shimla), needed an effusion. Thus, when the insurance policy meant for him by his grandmother was matured, Bond left for Britain in 1951 to live with his aunt. Meanwhile, Bond also knew that the English-publishing industry in India (as compared to the English scene), which would also be the scene as late as in the 1980s, was yet to be developed. Since much focus was being paid in text-book publishing during that period, almost no publisher showed interest in English fiction. Bond had to choose between possible recognition as a published author in Britain and his loyalty to India. Since young Bond had set out on his journey with an unforgettable memory of his motherland, he felt a tremendous urge to return to India soon after setting his feet in the West. Although professionally fruitful, this exile made him realise that the streets of Britain were not his cup of tea, and that Dehra's easy familiarity was far more conducive to personal growth. Britain, by any means, could never be his 'home'.

Claustrophobia and Homelessness in His 'Original Home'

'Oh India, my India, for all your dust there is blossom' (2012, 365), Bond wrote in his journal just before his voyage to Britain. Soon after he reached the West, the 17-year-old self wrote 'Lost', which would be his first published poem (1952) about how immensely his heart longed for India, and sent it to the then editor of *The Illustrated Weekly of India*, C.R. Mandy:

I boarded the big ship bound for the West,
The clean white liner,
In the noon-day heat
Coolies thronged the sun-drenched pier.
Yet I saw only
The village I had left,
And a boat at rest
On the river's shallow water
In the shade of the flowering
Long red-fingered poinsettia.
I saw not the big waves
But the ripple of running
Water in the reeds.

We came to London, lost in November mist:
In an ash-grey dawn at Tilbury dock

I longed for the warmth of a kiss
Of sunlight.

In the busy streets
Were cavalcades of people
Hurrying in a heat of hope.
But I saw only

The wheat-field, the tea-slope . . .
A cow at rest.
And longed for the soft, shoeless tread
Of a village boy . . . (2015)

The appeal of the poem, if we notice, reminds us of almost the same *upolobdhi* or understanding similar to what Amit Chaudhuri finds in Jibanananda Das's poetry. A few lines from Das's 'Rupasi Bangla' (Bengal the Beautiful) would be relevant to note in this context:

> You all go where you like—I shall stay here beside this Bengal bank—
> I'll see jackfruit-tree leaves losing hold at dawn, and at dusk a *shalik*'s
> brown wings turning cold—yellow-legged beneath some fair fluff it
> performs its bird-stride in dark in the grass—once—twice—all at once
> a *hijal* has cried from the forest for it to fly to its heart's stronghold ...
> (Chaudhuri 20, 275)

This is one of his repeatedly pronounced yearnings to return to his origin, Bengal. Das, agreeably the most significant Bengali poet after Tagore, who had never been outside the geographical space of Bengal for a considerable period of time, must have been irked by the intrusion of urban/unprecedented space (Kolkata) which he wistfully encountered for professional reasons. Now, the sense of being lost cannot be eradicated. Coming to our discussion, the pain of displacement in a foreign land was inevitable to Bond. It was Britain that was lacerating his heart by not being India; and London was choking him by not being Dehra. The emplacement far from everyone and everything known produces an emptiness. In this sojourn, alienation came to him as a lesson which he relearnt. This somewhat half-willing decision to plunge into English physicality leaving behind the growing-up space induced his sin of foreignness. It is why, the more Ruskin Bond felt the absence of India, the more he became obliged to vivify the country with tenacity, with the loss of Indian sound, colour, dust, emotion and heat, revealed in compelling details. It seems clear that the discontinuity of familiar atmosphere deepened his expatriation, and this perhaps enabled him to write, to borrow Salman Rushdie, 'properly and concretely on a subject of universal significance and appeal' (2012, 12). Bond's estrangement was more because he found the attitude of his aunt's family strange; instead of encouraging him, they constantly forced him to suppress his 'Indian' self and live like a British. Bond's projection of an Indianised identity through the characterisation of Rusty in *The Room on the Roof* (henceforth *The Room*), which I shall discuss in the next chapter, therefore denotes an Anglo-Indian's desire to be 'simply' an Indian.

What Bond confronted in Britain were the tribulations of many Anglo-Indians abroad. Britain was really an artificial embellishment upon which the Anglo-Indians' idea of home was imagined. The Anglo-Indians had expected that their sense of social and cultural which they experienced in India would be replaced by a feeling of homecoming in Britain. But much to their dismay, they felt alienated in their imaginary homeland and were thus caught in a sociocultural space, where the sense of not belonging anywhere became a stark reality. Bond's failure to adapt to a new environment induced in him a sense of social and cultural dislocation, which was very common among the exiled Anglo-Indians. Another significant aspect of their blindfolded Eurocentric affiliations is the fact that, as the Anglo-Indian scholar Alzena D'Costa seems a little protective about, Anglo-Indians, advertently or inadvertently, were ignorant of their emotional space that existed in their homeland, India (2006, 3). Commenting on the Anglo-Indian race, Herbert Stark maintains a similar opinion: 'We have our immediate interests vested in India, and we naturally identify ourselves with the social, economic, and political development and aspirations of our mother-country' (2015, 131–32). The Britain they had actually thought of with regard to an ideal locale of spatial belonging turned out to be a completely different reality, which brought them down to believe that they were moving about in an illusion. In India—their 'adopted' home, they had constructed an image of faraway physicality with so much passion and conviction that after entering the original reality, they were soon disillusioned. In addition, they were frustrated because they realised that the idea of future prospects in terms of working and economic conditions in Britain—which would possibly be subject to threat in independent India—was based on illusions. The irony was what they encountered could no longer be substituted with the erstwhile make-believe notion. Now despairing and marooned, Ruskin Bond's urge to get rid of this sense of loss was only possible by leaving the place and by reclaiming the India that dwelt in his sensibility. The act of fictionalising *The Room* partly fulfilled this reversion. Since he was physically removed from his homeland, there might have been a chance of losing precision in details, as Rushdie in his essay 'The Imaginary Homeland' indicates while highlighting the plight of diasporic writers. But because Bond was not reworking solely out of memory but consulting his journal entries, India in the authorial vision was not 'imaginary' but a deeply-felt reality. Out of these entries he 'produced a novel, raw, naïve and imperfect, but brimming with life and joy and truth, my own truth, for to be true to oneself is to be true to others' (Bond 2012, 412). Ruskin Bond's memory of India, moreover, was still fresh because he already started writing within a year or so. This act of re-treading may fairly be seen as a kind of reappraisal of his evolving identity, or from where his Anglo-Indianness is transformed into Indianness, or at least if he really has any hesitation at all.

Emily's family would treat Bond with pity as if they were taking care of a poor-White who had lost his father and whose mother, now remarried, failed to look after him. They were unsympathetic both towards his feelings for India and his literary ambition. Even though his maternal uncle, Dr John Heppolette, was a recognised South-Indian Christian doctor and Emily was an Anglo-Indian, Edith's act of remarrying an Indian, for them, was something that could not be accepted. The racial superiority his uncle strived to impose upon him would reflect on Rusty and Mr John Harrison's relationship in *The Room*. To Bond's detriment, they were strict in bringing him up in a more English way by, say, constantly urging him to stop corresponding with Indian friends, thereby trying to cut off the least possibility to 'connect' with his place of origin. This kind of 'colonial attitudes that still prevailed in my [his] uncle's family' (2012, 376) sickened the young mind and compelled him to state that 'they were the champions of Empire!' (376). Such an anti-Indian outlook not only distanced Bond from his relatives but intensified his sense of dislocation in the alien land. It is interesting to note that the inception of Rusty's critique of his guardian (Mr Harrison) has already been a subjective experience by the authorial identity. Although Bond's arriving at (North) London partly complemented the cosmopolitan ambience of Dehra, it could not reciprocate the affection and ease he was accustomed to. While moving to London from Jersey's 'insularity' (385), young Bond was accompanied by two books: while Charles Dickens's *The Pickwick Papers* (1836–37), a humorous account of companionship and innocence, must have moved Bond (besides its literary value) by its treatment of adventure—a living human phenomenon that constantly guides life, the other book, Richard Jefferies's autobiography *The Story of My Heart* (1883), talks about the soul's journey that yearns for human warmth. The motif of journey recurs in Bond's works frequently, signifying how we journey every living moment, without quite realising it, into human mysteries. Journey widens the corridors of self-reflection; Bond's act of carrying these books also suggests a metaphorical journey experienced by the authorial self.

Ruskin Bond, as hinted above, was lured to London also because it was a city of literary heroes of his 'bookish boyhood'. True that his life in London was liberating as compared to that of Jersey and the city did nurture his artistic vocation, but the longing to return never left him. It is also true that it was in London that he fell in love with a Vietnamese girl Vu-Phuong, was independent and socially active, and gave a few talks at BBC,[2] but his heart was strongly rooted in India. In his book *The India I Love* (2004), Bond retrospects:

> Most of my landladies were Jewish [in London]—refugees from persecution in pre-war Europe—and I too was a refugee of sorts, still very unsure of where I belonged. Was it England, the land of my father, or India, the land of my birth? But my father had also been born in India, had grown up and made a living there, visiting *his* father's land, England, only a couple of times during his life.
>
> The link with Britain was tenuous, based on heredity rather than upbringing. It was more in the mind. It was a literary England I had been drawn to, not a physical England. (59)

Since the sense of non-belongingness was ever present, the more he felt alienated inwardly the stronger was his urge to revert to his *desh*. Bond's expatriation can, therefore, be seen as an attempt to affirm his Indian self rather than, what Khorana also finds, '"recovering" his English identity' (2003, 26). In *Scenes*, the memoirist clarifies:

> Even though I had grown up with a love for the English language and its literature, even though my forefathers were British, Britain was not really my place. I did not belong to the bright lights of Piccadilly and Leicester Square; or, for that matter, to the apple orchards of Kent or the strawberry fields of Berkshire. I belonged, very firmly, to peepal trees and mango groves; to sleepy little towns all over India; to hot sunshine, muddy canals, the pungent scent of marigolds; the hills of home; spicy odours, wet earth after summer rain, neem pods bursting; laughing brown faces; and the intimacy of human contact. (2012, 385–86)

The Anglo-Indians strongly imagined themselves, as I have already discussed, to be culturally Europeans and 'as transnationals for whom "home" was in Britain' (Caplan 2001, 152). They were stuck in an imagined European existence, either heard or imagined, which they had never experienced before. Bond did not sojourn to Britain with the hope of settling abroad. Therefore, even though it was easier to get jobs and even though it was his ancestral root, the differences in terms of moral values, lack of warmth in human relationship, lifestyle, matter-of-fact daily office jobs and, above all, personal apathy made him feel that Britain was not really a land where 'home' could be re-established. The paradox lies in the fact that the West made Ruskin Bond feel how traumatic the effect of cultural isolation could be. His essentially inclusive Indian ethos, in many respects, clashed with an otherwise dissimilar attitude of the 'English' English lifestyle. In brief, Britain was not akin to his temperament:

> I knew I did not belong there and I disliked the place immensely. Within days of my arrival I was longing for the languid, easy-going, mango-scented air of small-town India: the gulmohur trees in their fiery summer splendour; barefoot boys riding buffaloes and chewing on sticks of sugarcane; a hoopoe on the grass, blue jays performing aerial acrobatics; a girl's pink dupatta flying in the breeze; the scent of wet earth after the first rain; and most of all my Dehra friends. (Bond 2012, 367–68)

Also, what Ruskin Bond perhaps suffered was the dearth of 'multiplicity of commingled faiths and cultures' conducive to create 'a remarkably secular ambience' (Rushdie 2010, 16), which he had experienced in Dehradun, or in other words, which his upbringing in India had infused in him. This absence was strongly felt particularly at his Aunt Emily's house. In his fictional debut (in terms of books) *The Room*, Rusty's moving away beyond the handcuff of Dehra's Anglo-Indian communal existence can legitimately be read as the authorial desire to see 'self' beyond any narrow order so as to be a part of a wider India, if not more. With Rusty, Bond looks into his heart and measures himself. The association with India by the authorial identity can better be seen in a laconic summation when Bond describes how his daily sense of confinement in Britain hindered his eternal allegiance with his homeland:

> When I was living in London as a young man in the 1950s, I was homesick and miserable, separated by a thousand miles of ocean, plain and desert from my beloved Himalayas. And then one morning the depressing London fog became a mountain mist, and the sound of traffic became the *hoo-hoo-hoo* of the wind in the branches of tall deodar trees. (2015, 44)

The Return from the Exile

In Britain, Ruskin Bond was exposed, what Ashis Nandy notes in a slightly different context, 'not to the Westernised lifestyle of the Indians but to the Western ways of the English' (1983, 89). To Bond, the West appeared to be too cold to be welcoming, too placid and reticent to be greeted. The experience was estranging and depressing; it was more than a cultural shock; it was, as it appears, something that curbs a young adult's will to survive. Anything he did in the land, alien to him, gave little comfort. Initially he was scared of surroundings and concerned how he would get rid of this; afterwards, it was about managing adequate money to guarantee a return ticket to India. The dream of becoming a published author was always there, but the trauma of displacement he underwent was even more intense. What the author's alter-ego expresses in *The Room*, 'inside of me, I am all lonely' (86) can aptly be aligned with the subjective predicament in Britain, which was an entirely different ambience for Bond. If there is any sense of ambivalence before his sojourn to Britain, the same sense of non-belongingness in Britain ascertained his true root in India. And, if his move to Britain is seen as an escape of an anglicised self, he did so to renew his outlook.

Curiously, instead of being at ease in his ancestral 'home' in Britain, Ruskin Bond's failure to adapt to the new environment resulted in sociocultural alienation delineating his exiled stature away from the familiar atmosphere. What he truly felt there can be summed up, borrowing from Edward Said, as an 'un healable rift forced between a human being and a native place, between the self and its true home' whose 'essential sadness can never be surmounted' (Said 2000, 173), until his immediate return to *swadesh*. Bond's predicament may better be comprehended if we try to analyse his emplacement as a culturally displaced identity, given the fact that he was born and brought up as a community member who is thought to be culturally inclined to Europe (or, Britain, to be more specific). This was what was common to many 'children of colonialism'.[3] Kipling felt almost the same; but what spared him is his conscious attempt to distinguish himself (as British) from Indians. Kipling writes in 'Shrine of the "Baba-Log"': 'I grew up in bright sunshine, I grew up with tremendous space, I grew up with animals, I grew up with excitement, I grew up believing that white people were superior' (1975, 21). Such racial superiority, which Kipling artfully mastered, was evident among some of the Anglo-Indians. Bond himself had witnessed this, for instance, in the attitudes of his maternal uncle in Jersey.

Necessarily, then, being wholly cut off from his native land, he is now in a cultural terrain only to get bewildered despite living there for three and a half years. The force of exile is so compelling, as explained by Said in his essay 'Reflection on Exile' (2000), that those who undergo it experience a sense of orphanhood. Despite his claim that '[e]xile is not, after all, a matter of choice: you are born into it, or it happens to you', Said implies its positive aspect (184). Far from being 'satisfied, placid, or secure' (186), exile unsettles its subject but allows him to revive his relations to the native place. It is now that the window of channelising his vexation is opened up, and objectifying it in fiction is followed. At this point of discussion, it is curious to note how *The Room on the Roof* is enriched circuitously. Thus, on the one side, the novelist's exiled-self makes his fictional alter-ego realise how firmly rooted his identity is in India, and on the other, while unriddling Rusty's predicament, the novelist is self-assessing his own.

In the case of Bond, the exilic condition could have been felt in India, his 'adopted home'. This contrary outcome signals that India is not just Bond's place of origin but becomes a site to accommodate his emotional space as well. Setting aside the unavoidable tensions as consequences of British imperialism, India stands out to be Bond's 'home'. If the vacillation between India and Britain was ever apparent in Bond's works, it can fairly be argued that Bond took this quandary of his self abroad and reverted to India leaving it behind.

Since the idea of homelessness works more on the psychic level than that of the physical, the memory of Dehra, in fact, gives Bond an idea of homing. Bond's critical shift from a familiar space to an unfamiliar one badly affects his coherence of living. Therefore, how the idea of 'home', ironically, stands from 'homelessness', can easily be gauged in Bond's subjective expression of his dissatisfaction to cope with the new environment in Britain. Bond's failure to re-establish 'home' in Britain also came from his fear of perpetual suspension of his personal resource, Dehra. The omission of everyday activities and intimacy at personal ground—eating *jalebis* at Dehra's street, or cycling with Sitaram for time unspecific is also home—amidst intellectual pursuit ached him. The amount of 50 pounds he received as advance against royalties from *Andre Deutsch*, his would-be publisher, along with a few savings from his daily job(s) and write-ups, Bond bought a ticket to return home. Saili, Bond's biographer, comments:

> The urge to leave had been so great, the wait had been so long, that he couldn't be sure of his good fortune. It was only when his ship had sailed into the Channel that he heaved a sigh of relief, smiled again, thumbed his nose at England, and allowed himself to feel a little affection for the miserable old city of London. (2004, 74)

Desh is *desh*; *videsh* cannot replace its authenticity. Neither can a soul be completely happy in *videsh*. In his journal *The Lamp Is Lit* (2012), Bond philosophises, '[h]appiness is an elusive state of mind, not to be gained by clumsy pursuit' (572). To Bond, *desh* is India, where all of its treasures are so finely blended in his heart that he cannot ignore it anyway. In the poem entitled 'This Land Is Mine' Bond's poetic assures himself: 'This land is mine/Although I do not own it,/This land is mine/ because I grew upon it' (2007, 121).

Exilic condition tends to produce a deep sense of nostalgia—a longing for 'lost' home becomes evident. If we try to examine the reason that incited young Bond to come back to India from his exile, lack of warmth in human relationship and unfamiliar environs of the foreign land appear in the forefront. The absence of Dehra's 'human contact' is the most predominant condition he missed in Britain, and this accentuated his yearning to revert to the dust he had long been acquainted with. Which is why, immediately after arriving home, he roamed in search of his favourite Dehra on Dipi's (Haripal's youngest brother) bicycle, as if to regain his broken tie, to restore his guilt-ridden soul with ever-present loyalty to a land that had given him an identity. Looking back in literary efflorescence, Ruskin Bond did not do what Tagore (once) did and regretted. In a letter to E.J. Thompson in 1921, Tagore wrote: 'My original vocation was as a mere Bengali poet. I know I am misinterpreting myself as a poet to western readers. Now I am becoming frightened of its enormity and am willing to make a confession of my misdeeds' (Chaudhuri 2018, 245). Even at that point, Bond was quite aware that his subject is India and his readers, primarily, are Indian, and therefore he held no confusion to misguide himself. Had he made it liberal, it could have been an advantage for his first novel in the Western readership, but in that case, he, like Tagore, would have misled himself from his pursuit. The social and cultural values of India had shaped his morale, taught him how to behave, act and think. In Britain, Bond felt guilty because he had left his homeland in hope of professional conveniences. Such perception of disloyalty was not uncommon among post-independent Anglo-Indian migrants (Williams 2002, 79). He felt guilty also because had he not been exiled, he might have flourished more as a human being as well as a writer amidst Dehra's affection, camaraderie and ease.

We can see why literary progress in Britain could not eliminate Bond's anguish. Not only did he miss his local friends immensely but he could also not make any close bonding in the UK. Athill, Bond's mentor, was sympathetic to this marooned boy, but Bond needed a camaraderie—a friendship that flowed from heart to heart. An almost 17-year-elder Athill thought she could be anything but a close friend to Bond. Had there been no Vu-Phoung, Bond would perhaps have left England earlier. He was in urgent need of a companion. The company of Vu-Phoung, whom he met at some party in London, partially comforted his alienation. Bond's love for her, followed by a marriage proposal, remained unrequited due to her sudden departure.

Besides *The Room*, a rapid examination of subjects he was writing about during the London days acquaints us with 'My Two Homes', a story dealing with an English boy's upbringing in an Indian home. While assessing someone's exilic state, we can sense its relevance and significance. The story, written in the Hampstead General Hospital where he was being diagnosed with a rare right-eye infection, aired in BBC's *Home Service Programme* soon after.

Ruskin Bond was already a cinephile—the habit developed in India at his father's encouragement. In 1951, the Jean Renoir movie, based on Rumer Godden's novel *The River* (1946), released in America; a year later it hit at a small cinema hall in St Helier (Jersey), which Bond meanwhile discovered. Ruskin Bond's desire for the Indian context was deeply aroused by its lyrical screen interpretation. Renoir's cinematic adaption was a celebration of India in all her magnificence, that, in Khorana's words, 'not only struck a responsive chord in Bond, but it prompted him to begin writing an intensely autobiographical first novel [. . .]' (2003, 27). Instead of presenting communal hostilities, the dilemma of migration, partition, religious conflicts, the movie declassed all sorts of colonial-colonised discourse and advocates a true humane connection. Renoir's painterly ability to communicate moved Bond so much so that he went to watch it a number of times.

The technicolour mode, experimented by the French director for the first time in his career, closely depicted the nuanced life of India to the Western audience. Renoir's treatment, without being biased on either side, was so sincere yet so sensitive that Bond must have felt how it captured the true mood of India. Further, the pictorial details of cinematography were in complete harmony with the land Bond could easily relate to.

It will be pertinent to say here a few words about what Godden had written and, in almost exact tone, Renoir had shown. In an upper-middle-class English family of Narayangunj (now in Bangladesh), Bogey is the third and only boy child to his parents. He is about ten years of age and his all-day-long companion is Kanu, a poor Indian boy of the same age. Bewitched by a snake-enchanter, Bogey intends to learn the art of taming a cobra with a flute. Bogey, quite ignorant of life threat and in the absence of elders, arranges for a flute and starts taming a cobra in a giant banyan tree at a corner of their palatial house. Kanu, who finds Bogey's act enticing, accompanies him curiously. In spite of two different vernacular languages used by these two friends, their bonding comes out impressively, reinforcing that language or class can barely be an impediment to true friendship. The Indian-European camaraderie as shown in the movie must have touched sensitive Bond. However, one tragic day, Bogey loses his life while taming the serpent; Kanu out of fear runs away when Harriet, the central character and one of Bogey's elder sisters tries to ask about her brother's whereabouts. Kanu's suffering and helplessness are equally depicted when Bogey's dead body is taken away in a coffin for the burial ceremony. Their closeness is so convincingly filmed, as against cultural-racial animosity governed to lacerate human bonding, that it must have re-lived Bond's own childhood experiences in India. Such interpretation, far from being misleading and exotic, not merely instigated Bond to revert to India but also made him proud to be an Indian, to belong to the country that prioritises humanity amidst hundreds of cultural, social, racial or religious differences.

At this point of time, back to our discussion, Ruskin Bond was so sensitive about India that he was immediately disappointed after watching a Hindi film called *Aan* (Pride), India's first technicolour movie. Unlike *Aan* (1952), which gave a 'completely misleading and over-romanticised conception of India' (Bond 2014, 149), Renoir's *The River* harmonised its setting with human compassion. The telling of Renoir's film is poetic. From the very outset, Renoir has been sincere to his method. Although the original text centres around Harriet, the adolescent alter-ego of Rumer Godden, who will eventually come to awareness through experiences, the cinematic adaptation, besides upholding this, focuses on larger spheres, where, for instance, we witness Melanie, a girl of inter-racial ethnicity, and Bogey, who loosely resembles Bond's own childhood image.

The characterisation of Anglo-Indian Melaine, which was conceived by Godden (who was also the screenplay writer of this film) after learning firsthand 'of the white hostility toward those who mixed with Indians' (Christie, n.pag.), is something which possibly led young Bond to reconsider:

> The very suggestion of romance between Melanie and the white American, Captain John, challenged racial taboos on both sides of the Atlantic, and the character of Melanie, who is not in the book, was devised precisely to give an Indian other than a servant an authentic voice and presence in the film's central drama. (Christie 2015, n.pag.)

Added to this, any question regarding whether Melanie's easy fraternity both with Indians and Europeans in Narayangunj could have aroused in Bond any racial dilemma is insignificant. When Mr John, Melanie's father, Renoir has shown, agonises over Melanie's mixed-race status, the daughter mildly questions him:

> —Why did you send me to a Western school?
> —Because you have Western inheritance too. It's a puzzle. I don't know where you belong. Sometimes I think I put you in an afraidful position. Perhaps you never should have been born.
> —But I am born. Someday I shall find out where I belong.

The depiction of Anglo-Indians' natural mixing with local Indians seemed to inspire Bond and brought him back to Dehra's *raga* he had once left. There might have been mutual incomprehension in a few instances, but the movie lends a positive note:

> None of the principal characters in *The River* find immediate happiness; instead, they learn to overcome frustration and despair in a series of experiences that we can perhaps see as therapeutic but that are also influenced by the philosophy of Hinduism. The Europeans who are the main protagonists of *The River* participate in the Hindu rituals, such as Dewali, as observers rather than believers. Yet when their greatest challenge comes, with young Bogey's death, they adopt some of the trappings of Hindu ritual and much of its stoicism. One aspect of Hindu theology in particular seems to have fascinated Renoir—the goddess Kali's cyclical path from destruction to rebirth—and this could be seen as the film's overall theme. (Christie 2015, n.pag.)

Set in Narayangunj, a river country by the mighty Brahmaputra (Shitalakshya, a distributary of the Brahmaputra, to be more specific), the novel, which Bond read after watching the film, is written with such wide-eyed observation and child-like innocence that it immediately kindled Bond's nostalgia. The autobiographical elements are merged so credibly that Narayangunj immediately becomes a prototype of India. Furthermore, Renoir's adaptation, much like the original text, is one such endearing instance that enabled young Bond to see the quaint side of the debated and counter-debated world of colonial India. The impact of this lyrical movie during the days of separation was so self-revealing on Bond's exiled self that it must have incited him to associate passionately with the landscape of Dehra. Thus, Dehra turned out to be a concrete, identifiable cultural locale, which was no less important for an 'Indian' craving wistfully from the distant seashore.

Even though there was no certainty in making a fortune in India in English writing, even though the publication of his first novel was still an event in the future, 21-year-old Bond reverted to his homeland, against the current of Anglo-Indian migration, with another dream—either to be fulfilled or failed. Let us for a moment concentrate on the idea of home. Avtar Brahtheorises it:

> . . . as the site of everyday lived experience. It is a discourse of locality, the place where feelings of rootedness ensue from the mundane and the unexpected of daily practice. Home here connotes our networks of family, kin, friends, colleagues and various other 'significant others'. It signifies the social and psychic geography of space that is experienced in terms of a neighbourhood or a home town. That is, a community 'imagined' in most part through daily encounters. This 'home' is a place with which we remain intimate even in moments of intense alienation from it. It is a sense of 'feeling at home'. (2004, 4)

Ruskin Bond's preference for better economic and professional opportunities to be fulfilled by Britain is nonetheless a political move. But this act is not with the loss of faith in India—the collective whole of one's social, cultural, political and spiritual spatiality. Therefore, behind this somewhat legitimated political practice called exile exits a kind of exploration of a different (and ancestrally likened to) geographical space and its negotiation with the habituated space of his mind. But, Bond's perception of space, having grown up in India, fails to find a suitable equivalent outside the habituated sociocultural sphere. The rift between the habituated sense of belonging with the emotional space in India and its failure to find an equivalent sense of possession in a new geographical space complicates his idea of home.

Seen alternatively, Bond undertook a journey to *videsh* with a dream, partly fulfilled his dream of getting acquainted with literary England and returned to his *desh* with another dream. His sojourn proved fruitful in terms of literary fruition, while wide readership was yet to come mainly from Indian readers. On the one hand, this is literally a journey where Ruskin Bond moves from place to place, job to job, before discovering his true calling. On the other hand, it is a metaphoric journey to find his true origin: 'It was only by going away that I came to the realisation that I would never go away again, no matter what happened. This was where I belonged and this was where I would stay, come flood or fury' (2012, 263).

In 1951, Bond sailed to Britain to seek his fortune—more keenly to dig into his own self, and in 1955, when the immigrant waves were still much in the air, he reverted to India to answer himself, even when the uncertainty about his fortune in this newly independent country remained undismissed. *Scenes from a Writer's Life* (2012) chronicles this entire journey. It will, therefore, not be a misreading if Bond's return to the 'sensuous welcoming arms' of India is considered as an act to get over dislocation. Ruskin Bond's return from *videsh* to *desh* connotes his urge to identify himself with Indian physicality; it lends no hastiness but an understanding which, once troubled his adolescent self, now becomes evident in exile. That is to say, the sojourn to Britain un riddles the traumatic ambivalences of an Anglo-Indian by answering numerous questions and rendering a renewed self-awareness. The entire journey is literalised in *Scenes*, where the authorial identity overcomes his inner-conflicts to affirm: '"I am an Indian"—in the broadest, all-embracing, all-Indian sense of the word' (263). If the absence of a personal sense of geography ensued by the dearth of familial atmosphere directs him to India, his attachment with the familial space compensates for the vacuum. In the next three chapters I will discuss the progress of Bond's textual selves, and how with time they negotiate with and react to the older ones.

Notes

1. The interview was taken on 6 April 2016 by the author of the book at Landour.
2. BBC producer Prudence Smith invited him to give a few talks on Radio's Third Programme. For more, see Bond's *The India I Love*.
3. The expression 'children of colonialism' refers to the Anglo-Indians in this present study. For more, see Lionel Caplan's *Children of Colonialism: Anglo-Indians in a Postcolonial World* (2003).

Bibliography

Bhabha, Homi K. 1992. 'The World and the Home'. *Social Text*, 31/32: 141–53. Available at: JSTOR (accessed on 9 May 2015).

Blunt, Alison. 2005. *Domicile and Diaspora: Anglo-Indian Women and the Spatial Politics of Home*. Oxford: Blackwell.

Bond, Ruskin. 1994. *The Best of Ruskin Bond*. New Delhi: Penguin. n.pag. Available at: Archive.org (accessed on 17 April 2015).

———. 2004. *The India I Love*. New Delhi: Rupa.

———. 2007. 'This Land Is Mine'. *Book of Verse*. Gurgaon: Penguin.

———. 2008. *A Town Called Dehra*. New Delhi: Penguin.

———. 2010. 'The Room on the Roof'. *Classic Ruskin Bond Vol 1: The Novels*. New Delhi: Penguin, 1–114.

———. 2012. 'Scenes from a Writer's Life'. *Classic Ruskin Bond Vol. 2: The Memoirs*. Delhi: Penguin Books, 253–404.

———. 2012. 'The Lamp Is Lit'. *Classic Ruskin Bond Vol. 2: The Memoirs*. New Delhi: Penguin, 405–575.

———. 2014. *Love among the Bookshelves*. Haryana: Penguin.

———. 2015. *A Book of Simple Living: Brief Notes from the Hills*. New Delhi: Speaking Tiger.

Brah, Avtar. 1996. *Cartographies of Diaspora: Contesting Identities*. London: Routledge.

Caplan, Lionel. 1995. '"Life is only abroad, not here" the Culture of Emigration among Anglo-Indians in Madras', *Immigrants and Minorities*, 14(1): 26–46. Available at: *Taylor & Francis Online* (accessed on 12 May 2015).

———. 2001. *Children of Colonialism: Anglo-Indians in a Postcolonial World*. Oxford: Berg.

———. 2003. 'Colonial and Post-Colonial Hybridities: Eurasians in India'. *IIAS Newsletter* 30: 16. Available at: http://iias.asia/sites/default/files/IIAS_NL30_16.pdf (accessed on16 May 2016).

Chaudhuri, Amit. [2008] 2012. *Clearing a Space: Reflections on India, Literature and Culture*. New Delhi: Penguin.

———. 2018. *The Origins of Dislike*. New Delhi: Oxford University Press.

Christie, Ian. 2015. 'The River: A New Authenticity'. *The Criterion Collection*. 20 April, n.pag. Available at: https://www.criterion.com/current/posts/357-the-river-a-new-authenticity (accessed on 15 May 2016).

D'Costa, A. 2006. 'Anglo-Indian Nostalgia: Longing for India as Homeland', *Second Annual Rhizomes: Re-visioning Boundaries Conference of The School of Languages and Comparative Cultural Studies*, February, Brisbane, Australia. Unpublished conference paper. The University of Queensland, 1–11. Available at: https://espace.library.uq.edu.au/view/UQ:7724/adc_rhiz.pdf (accessed on 13 February 2016).

Khorana, Meena G. 2003. *The Life and Works of Ruskin Bond*. Westport, CT: Praeger.

Kipling, Rudyard. 1975. 'Shrine of the "Baba-Log"'. In *Plain Tales from the Hills: Images of British India in the Twentieth Century*, edited by Charles Allen. London: Andre Deutsch Limited and the British Broadcasting Corporation.

Nandy, Ashis. 1983. *The Intimate Enemy: Loss and Recovery of the Self under Colonialism*. New Delhi: Oxford University Press.

Renoir, Jean. Dir. *The River*. United Artists, 1951. Film.

Rushdie, Salman. 2010. *Imaginary Homelands: Essays and Criticism 1981–1991*. London: Vintage.

Said, Edward W. 2000. *Reflections on Exile and Other Essays*. Cambridge: Harvard University Press, n.pag. Available at: Google Book Search (accessed on 12 January 2015).

Saili, Ganesh. 2004. *Ruskin, Our Enduring Bond*. New Delhi: Roli Books.

Stark, Herbert Alick. 2015. *Hostages to India*. Chennai: Anglo-Ink.

Williams, Blair. 2002. *Anglo-Indians: Vanishing Remnants of a Bygone Era*. New Jersey: CTR Inc. Available at: Google Book Search (accessed on 9 February 2016).

3

Intervening the Self

Developing the Consciousness of Rusty in *The Room on the Roof*

The Room on the Roof (henceforth *The Room* in this chapter) is the textualisation of the authorial identity's psychological necessity towards introspection. This is where the novelist, through his hero, presents a mind trapped between two contradictory outlooks. This novel recounts an adolescent's journey, in which Ruskin Bond assesses his own desires as a teenager and his dreams of becoming a free Indian national. At the centre of the story is Anglo-Indian Rusty, who, orphaned in his childhood, is educated by Mr John Harrison, his father's cousin. But their relationship is far from being amiable. Rusty's sudden acquaintance with some boys of Dehra's (now Dehradun) bazaar—a strict 'no' to him—defers but solidifies his evolving relationship with his country, India. It will be an interesting study to see how Rusty responds to the pluralism that Dehra's bazaar produces.

This coming-of-age narrative details the tribulations and ambitions of the introvert but adventurous Rusty, who lives with his guardian on the outskirts of Dehra, a north-Indian town which once served as a reclusive hub for Europeans during the colonial period. Born and brought up in India, yet trapped within the enclosure of his community's outlook, Rusty's inquisitive mind strives, the text insinuates, to perceive the world outside. His life takes a different turn when he comes in contact with the diverse Indian atmosphere of Dehra's bazaar. Subsequent events lead towards self-doubts and self-discovery of the protagonist: underneath Rusty's apathy towards his guardian's strict order lies his wish to find a 'room' of his own in Dehra's extraordinary multiplicity. The word 'room' of the title serves a metaphoric purpose both to the novelist and to his fictional representation, connoting a quest for 'home' or personal 'space', which must not be pre-conditioned and regulated by preset notions. This chapter will discuss how the boy manages to locate his space in a democratic setting, thereby ameliorating his identity-seeking concerns.

Literature, written by children and young adults, often finds a common consensus that it should be received lightly. That the child has cognitive intelligence—aided with inborn talent and creative brilliance—is often categorically spurned. This is exactly what happened to young Bond in his school days. His first manuscript, written at the age of thirteen, sentimentalises his teenage life during of an annual school term. *Nine Months*, as it was named, remains unpublished because it was destroyed on the ground of piquing snobbery of some of the faculty members of Bishop Cotton School, Shimla, where Bond was a student of the eighth standard. His first book *The Room on the Roof*, written at the age of seventeen, must have brought a smashing rejoinder to the stereotyped idea pointed out above.[1] Fictionalised from personal journal entries in Britain under the editorial suggestions of Diana Athill of *Andre Deutsch*, this novel celebrating his adolescent days of Dehra before exile could have easily stirred the literary landscape of adolescent fiction writing had the genre been recognised at that time. Ever since its first publication, no expression has been changed or revised in the successive editions and reprints of the novel. It seems that Ruskin Bond does not want to divert his readers from the perspective of his growing-up self; the novelist's unwillingness to further alteration in later editions ascertains his faith that the children/young-adult perspective is no less persuasive. Bond seems totally aware that children's literature is somewhat marginalised; hence he takes an opportunity to drive his point home through the preface to the book's 2016 edition published by Penguin India, to commemorate the sixtieth anniversary of the book's publication: 'What makes it "different", I think, is that it is a novel about adolescence by an adolescent; and for this reason I have never changed a word or made any revisions. It reflects the writer as he was when he wrote it—naïve, trustful, eager for love and friendship' (2016, xi).

'Bond is at his best when he deals with the dilemma of an adolescent', Prabhat K. Singh evaluates in his introduction to the edited volume *The Creative Contours of Ruskin Bond* (12). While dealing with the young-adult theme, it is fairly obvious that Bond manages a vivid picture of emotional and psychological intimacy. If he has to deal with a troubled childhood, he goes on to delineate Rusty's anguishing self-questioning with such close scrutiny that it immediately problematises the author-narrator/author-protagonist position. As is often the case, Bond's failure to deviate from subjective concerns is replicated in his inception of this insecure and somewhat confused state of Rusty's growing-up-identity as a justification of the author-narrator's vacillated youth. When written, it is necessary to mention that the novel (like most of his works) aims at uncategorised readership. Among Bond's works, *The Room* stands out strong not because of its wide circulation and international recognition but due to its engrossing depiction of a 16-year-old boy's deep-felt angst in the light of the colonial agenda of the ruling British in India. Rusty feels an urge to resolve his identity-dilemma because he is trapped in liminality between his Indian self and English one. His positioning amidst these two poles deepens his sense of vexation. The Anglo-Indian sense of anxiety of not truly belonging anywhere, therefore, recurs in the text in order to be frequently interrogated. In a way, *The Room* testifies two selves of Rusty: Rusty's identity as an Anglo-Indian elite ascribed by his community is contrasted with the identity that is subsequently formed out of individual choice. We notice Rusty negotiating to cope with his divided self-ensued partly by his dual-inheritance and partly by the colonial biases of his stern guardian.

Although he is asked to pursue an 'exclusive' Anglo-Indian life, he is rather fascinated by the democratic Indian consciousness—conducive to self-fulfilment—that might enable him to appreciate life outside the ghettoised Anglo-Indian barricade of Dehra. The present chapter deals with Rusty's wavering between two contradictory poles, which defers but determines individuation.

The novel is set in the languorous Dehra of 1950–51. The town's cosmopolitan fabric, far from being suspended by the singularity of thoughts, communicates multicultural spaces. Bond's Dehra is tolerant and sympathetic, so are his characters based on the town. Therefore, when an adolescent feels lonely and dejected, he is provided with a group of energetic friends, as compared to the 'dull' state of Rusty, to fulfil the vacuum. Rusty, at this point, seems only curious to know life outside the repressed order of his community. The narrative thus encompasses Rusty's dissatisfaction with his ghettoised identity and closeness to *desi* customs. This is the crux of the novel. This also helps the narrative to travel from one side of the bazaar to the other, from the colonial terrain to a postcolonial one, from rigidity to enlightenment, from claustrophobia to personal contentment. It is also found that Rusty's leap from his reclusive quasi-Englishness to emerge as a responsible and free Indian citizen, promises him better scope to understand life.

Self in Anglo-Indian Exclusivity

In *Culture and Imperialism*, Edward Said observes that '[p]artly because of empire, all cultures are involved in one another; none is single and pure, all are hybrid, heterogeneous, extraordinarily differentiated, and unmonolithic' (Said 1994, xxix). A child of the changing time, Ruskin Bond seems to register this heterogeneity in the postcolonial condition. It is therefore likely that Rusty is conceived to step in, interrogate, and seek an answer for his own mixed-racial identity. We must not forget that cultural amalgamation in British India gave birth to a minority community which gradually became known as Anglo-Indian. Although initially, their existence did not engender much anguish, it was towards the end of the British empire, especially from the 1930s, that this community encountered a sense of imminent orphanage, which increased considerably after the Indian independence. The condition was embedded deep in their psyche forever. As a representative of this group, Rusty's negotiation with his mixed-racial status is complex. He has to undergo a myriad of queries until his psychological tussle between his communal loyalty and individual choice finds a credible way to offer his highly-contested belonging an understanding. Said's usage of the expression 'unmonolithic' is significant insofar as it mandates zero privilege to colonial glory; instead, it inverts the slightest preference to colonial/authoritarian tools such as English education, whiteness, class-consciousness, Christianity and several other related ideologies. With this subversion, equal favour of indigenous culture, regional beliefs and values, local lifestyles and other so-long-subjugated elements are stressed upon.

As the story begins, we notice Rusty, a pale, blue-grey-eyed, fair-haired, shy boy walking alone in the rain until Somi, an Indian Sikh of the same age, offers him a free-ride on his bicycle. When their first meeting ends with an exchange of names, Somi casually invites Rusty for a meal at the bazaar's *chaat* shop. Meanwhile, during the ride, Somi introduces Rusty to Ranbir and Suri, the other two local friends, who are accommodated on the same bicycle. Rusty is impressed by Somi's warm, accommodating nature. The atmospheric rain, on the other hand, symbolises human bonding and promises a fresh start for Rusty.

Mr Harrison, a businessman by profession, is a stern and often indifferent 'official' guardian to young Rusty. His proprietary way of dealing with and absolute dismissal of any possibility of communication with the adolescent, intimidates Rusty. The warmth and concern that is normally associated with the word 'guardian' is wholly missing in Mr Harrison, thereby stifling Rusty's natural curiosity and exuberance: 'He

(Mr Harrison) seldom answered the boy's questions, and his own were stated, not asked; he proved and suggested, sharply, quickly, without ever encouraging loose conversation. He never talked about himself; he never argued: he would tolerate no argument' (Bond 2010, 8). Mr Harrison has educated the boy in 'an expensive school in the hills that was run on "exclusively European lines"' (8–9), and thus spent a handsome amount in the upbringing of his ward. As a result, he expects complete loyalty, howsoever forceful it may sound, from his ward. Rusty's anxiety in pleasing his guardian and proving his unquestioned loyalty to him, creates an identity trauma that flavours the first few sections of the book. What accentuates the crisis is the unwritten law of obeisance to his guardian's world view. The boy's life, as depicted in the initial pages of the text, is a life guided by Mr Harrison's outlook. Rusty is instructed not to play with the sweeper boy, the low-class untouchable, of their house because a 'servant' cannot be a friend to a *sahib*/'master'. The class discrepancy is inculcated into Rusty in such a way that he hesitates to accept the boy—the only other European of their community—as his playmate. This extreme class consciousness in the secluded part of Dehra is further articulated by the missionary's wife (of whom little is told): 'Even if you [Rusty] were an Indian, my child, you would not be allowed to play with the sweeper boy' (9). The master-servant dialectics confuses Rusty, as he wonders, if not him, who, then, would be the sweeper's boy's playmate. Like any sensitive child, Rusty, despite his cultural conditioning of discriminating against the sweeper's boy, finds it difficult to justify such bias. Later we would see how this class insulation is disrupted by Rusty's first experience in the bazaar.

A closer probe offers that Mr Harrison's way of rearing his ward, retaining his racial outlook, resembles the ploy of master/slave and coloniser/colonised binary—Rusty has been brought up by his guardian, so he is owned by him. Despite the fact that the rich European families in colonial India (even during the early years of post-independent India) would send their children abroad or to schools run by Europeans or at least to restrict their children from hobnobbing with their servants lest they be spoiled, the additional reference written in the text bears enough evidence about the harsh guardianship meted to Rusty. The boy's obeisance is most likely built out of deference to Mr Harrison's threatening demeanour, ginger moustache and the threat of corporal punishment with the 'supple malacca cane'. Even though Rusty has always obeyed his guardian and kept himself away from 'inferior' Indians, he subsequently subverts class consciousness by sharing a bicycle ride with Somi and others. Furthermore, Rusty's queries, which remain almost always unanswered, prepare him to question his guardian's 'legal' positioning in particular.

Though not discussed in details nor properly substantiated, but there appears an apparent pathology of superiority in Mr Harrison. He is obsessed with retaining a segregated elite lifestyle and an 'English' outlook. Mr Harrison is, in fact, the only and the finest negatively-depicted montage of all the real-life personalities Ruskin Bond fears or dislikes: his stepfather, Mr Hari; his maternal uncle in Jersey and Mr Fisher, the headmaster at Bishop Cotton School. Little is written about Mr Harrison; the novelist does not bother to offer much about him to his readers. Whatever is revealed projects him as a stern imperial follower, who blindly follows colonial codes, disfavours 'natives', and rules his economically and emotionally shackled ward. One thing, however, seems certain. Their relation is not allowed to go beyond master-ward equation. Even when he knows that Rusty has no other place to stay, he never feels sorry for the boy. Nor does he try to pursue him out of elderly concern. Later in the text, Mr Harrison's confrontation with Rusty at the entrance of the bazaar reveals that his life in the tea-estate business goes as usual, and there is no moral questioning on his part at seeing Rusty out of the shelter. Once he had wanted to keep dreamy Rusty under control, but now out of his control zone, he can only release his temper by informing the news of 'kicking the sweeper boy out of his house' for no offence (Bond 2010, 72). Since the story is almost always centred around Rusty, it is difficult to guess the level of frustration that Mr Harrison has in mind with the betrayal done by the British against the Anglo-Indians. What can be gauged is his elitism whether be it his way of looking at life or his clear motive to keep a distance from the 'natives'. Such obvious colonial bias may contribute to the evaluation of the inception of the Anglo-Indian identity. In *Britain's Betrayal in India* (1969), Frank Anthony informs us:

> Brought into existence deliberately by the British, used throughout British Indian history to serve and often to save British imperial interests, treated for the most part in a churlish manner, this comparatively microscopic Community, which has forged a not negligible, and in many respects, a notable history, was cynically betrayed by Britain before it withdrawal from India. (ii)

The European section of Dehra that we are so far familiar with does not appear to be free from colonial ideology. Even after the British Empire's departure from their wealthiest colony, Mr Harrison is enamoured by the imperial ideology. His English-style house with 'neat front gardens and nameplates on the gates' betokens an endeavour to oust all indigenous associations: 'The surroundings [of Mr John Harrison's house] on the whole were so English that the people often found it difficult to believe that they lived at the foot of the Himalayas, surrounded by India's thickest jungles. India started a mile away, where the bazaar began' (Bond 2010, 9). Mr Harrison is, in fact, more 'Anglo' than 'Indian'—a tragic hybrid of colonialism, and thus his ever-conscious 'exclusivity' never allows any space to embrace the local culture. Considering the post-1947 temporal space of heightened decolonisation, Elleke Boehmer in her book notices that nationalist opposition to colonial attitudes was very strong worldwide:

> From the 1920s onwards, but mightily in the 1950s, nationalist groups gave support to distinctly more combative political methods: non-cooperation; concerted demands for, as Gandhi phrased it in 1930,

> 'purnaswaraj' (complete independence); active resistance on all fronts, economic, cultural, and political, with the option for some nationalist movements of armed struggle. (2005, 174)

Relegating the 'diminishing European community' to the fringes of Dehra can, therefore, be realised from nationalist behaviour of the time. The expression 'diminishing' captures our attention as it implies decolonisation of indigenous culture from the clutch of European/colonial discourse, thereby reducing its strength and scope. Mr John Harrison, as an inheritor of colonial preconceptions, is a representative of this gradually decreasing minority community. The omniscient narrator writes:

> The community consisted mostly of elderly people, the others had left soon after Independence. These few stayed because they were too old to start life again in another country, where there would be no servants and very little sunlight; and though they complained of their lot and criticized the government, they knew their money could buy them their comforts; servants, good food, whisky, almost anything—except the dignity they cherished the most . . . (Bond 2010, 10)

However, aside from the fact that class-prejudice had not altogether vanished, the whole community cannot be accused of it because the essence of Anglo-Indian consciousness has partially been fashioned by 'Indian nationalist rhetoric' (D'Costa 2006, 3) and their communal distinctiveness has been misread on numerous occasions. It reminds us of the historical reference, noted by Lionel Caplan in his book: '[F]rom the Mutiny down to the present Anglo-Indians have upheld British prestige and proved themselves worthy of the [British] blood that flows in their veins' (2001, 98). In *The Room*, however, what strikes one immediately is the narrative objectivity in drawing the lifestyle of the community, and Rusty's reaction to it. The novelist's perspective unequivocally presupposes the adolescent's indifference towards their way of living, irrespective of any sociocultural or political conditioning, in independent India. Amidst the hangover of the mixed-racial issue, Rusty senses that he himself has to sort out his double-bind—his obligation to his community and his desire to associate with the wider current of his country—to attain an individual subjectivity. As a sensitive and concerned youth, Rusty perceives his dilemma and the necessity, I propose, of an alternative identification that can direct him to his future purpose in his motherland. Caplan's finding is relevant here: '[t]he Anglo-Indian with the superiority complex will find that the India of tomorrow has no need for him, while the Anglo-Indian who has learned to respect his Indian brother will discover that the future has a definite place and purpose for him' (2001, 102). Discontent with the essentialised racial myths, Rusty appears to imagine that his penchant towards Indianisation and his inclination to choose Dehra's culturally heterogeneous bazaar might resolve this bind by extracting him from the insularity of an 'exclusive' European self. This 'choice' for the bazaar is an outcome of great deliberation, as it stems from a dilemma—albeit forcefully or indecisively. Rusty is visibly at ease outside the conformity of his guardian's 'disciplinary' upbringing probably because it provides him liberty to examine the mind. The text explores that the given capacity to investigate, to see within, is easily possible when the boy connects with the physicality of bazaar reality. The literalisation of the novelist's desire for sensual India and to, perhaps unknown to himself, understand where the self finds ease becomes evident.

Rusty may initially be counted as a scapegoat of British colonial rhetoric—one whose birth and upbringing is designed by the imperial disregard of Anglo-Indian existence. Mr Harrison's house[2] with its power politics confuses Rusty; the house is too restrictive to favour any of the boy's opinions. Mr Harrison's house is incompatible for any mature self-realisation. Instead, the place hyphenates the idea of home in Rusty's mind. In *The Room*, 'home' serves a key motif, and Rusty's ceaseless chase for home results from the sense of homelessness, despite his sheltered existence in the Harrison house. While the absence of parental care and familial atmosphere makes his life irksome, Dehra's Indian bazaar, at this crucial juncture, partly fulfils the absence of a safe haven. To Rusty, home is not a mere physicality but a far meaningful connotation filled with privacy, security and freedom. In fact, the idea of home goes much beyond any geographical reach and entails spatial belongingness by attributing ease of living. In the process, Rusty finds his new home in Dehra's bazaar—be it the *chaat* shop, or Somi's house, or the room on the roof of the Kapoor family. From a subjective perspective, Dehra is also 'home' because it lends the novelist a constant reminder of the continued presence of his deceased father. Bond's later stay in Maplewood Cottage and then Ivy Cottage may be read as a constant attempt to retain a homely sense of living in their tranquil ambience, which Dehra once offered. In this context, Dehra's openness may not substitute parental care but can create a space akin to his temperament. Though the missionary's wife is affectionate, parental concern cannot be substituted by mere affection; nor can affection alone generate a homely feeling. The trope of Dehra as a familiar cultural locale is thus quite significant here: Rusty's identification with Dehra's openness is stronger than the suppressed life of the Anglo-Indian community. This is validated by the textual hint in the very first page: 'The further he could get from Dehra,[3] the happier he was likely to be' (Bond 2010, 1).

Breaking the Decorum: Resisting the Colonial Prejudice of Mr Harrison

Underneath a naïve account of an impulsive teenager, *The Room* is a layered narrative which sparkles with diverse perspectives, and with each fresh reading, it unsettles the reader by adding something new and deep for its meaning. On the surface, the novel portrays a sensitive orphan's struggle and his dealing with his insensitive guardian; but, on the deeper order, it addresses and attempts to neutralise race-class dichotomy, which has long been active in the Anglo-Indian community as a colonial hangover. Since Dehra's European community favours communal exclusivity, Rusty is not entirely free from its effect. Mr Harrison's stubbornness in pursuit of colonial glory, even on a domestic plane, colours the earliest imaginings of the boy. He leaves no stones unturned to inculcate ideas of a racial breach and class discrepancy in Rusty. It is why Mr Harrison's concern as an ideal guardian is far from being credible. On the contrary, this lack of latitude rather allows one to characterise him only in a political dimension. It is also ironic that the guardian's house, far from generating the idea of home, serves as a site of colonial reinforcement to mould his ward's mind.

In Dehra's bazaar, Rusty can observe the cardinal realities which are otherwise removed from Dehra's Anglo-Indian hub. With textual progression, we notice Rusty's gradual awareness of both the restricted laws prevalent in his community and the bazaar's secular drive where class, colour and caste differences intermingle. Mr Harrison's short-sightedness to accept India as his own country comes out of his ignorance of the imperial strategy, in which his own identity is trapped and polarised. Either he is misunderstood or he is found channelising his angst by allying himself with the coloniser's attitude. Whatever the reason may be, he seems unaware of his own position, or perhaps, he is too willing to get rid of the confusion of his liminal positioning. Rusty's enchantment with the bazaar-activities is thus set against Mr Harrison's deliberate misunderstanding of the cultural values of the land.

Consequently, Dehra's bazaar is emphasised in the text rather than the isolated European part of the town. The bazaar is further prioritised because it, the narrative suggests, never conforms to the colonial discourse of the neat European section. Although it contests Rusty's Eurocentric affiliations, it provides him ample space to amalgamate diverse Indian customs so far undiscovered. If the bazaar is viewed as a potent agency of resistance against the English pretentiousness triggered by Mr Harrison, Rusty's involvement with it entails an attempt at overcoming the effect of mental colonisation inflicted upon him. In fact, Dehra's Indian bazaar, situated on the 'other side' of the Clock Tower, resembles a 'wholly recovered "reality", free of all colonial taint' (Tiffin 1995, 95). The place is fraught with local experiences—a practical dissent against colonial mores of any kind. Resistance in this text works primarily through disregard accorded to colonial privileges and the emphasis on local practices. Postcolonial critic, Bill Ashcroft reminds us:

> [I]f we think of resistance as any form of defence by which an invader is 'kept out', the subtle and sometimes even unspoken forms of social and cultural resistance have been much more common. It is these subtle and more widespread forms of resistance, forms of saying 'no', that are most interesting because they are most difficult for imperial powers to combat. (2001, 20)

Although Rusty's visit to Dehra's bazaar after ignoring his guardian's strict warning constitutes the first major step to surmount his guardian's set of ideas, prioritizing individual choice, his entrance is a pitiful beginning. Somi, the Sikh boy whom Rusty has met earlier, cycles at a good speed until his way is blocked by Maharani, the queen of the bazaar cows. To protect the sacred cow, he swings clear of Maharani but collides with Rusty. As a result of that Rusty, to his utter displeasure, finds himself thrown into a bazaar gutter, which is mere 'vegetable discharge' to Somi. The preference shown to Maharani over Rusty, by the Indian boy, super imposes the Hindu belief (even though Somi is a Sikh)over an 'English' boy's religious belief. Apart from the obvious significance of choice, it is also a way of challenging Rusty's fixed notions. Again, once Rusty walks into this 'forbidden' zone, the bazaar with its filth, dust, smell, crowd, beggars and cacophony unsettles his English decency. The smell of rotten vegetables disturbs his habituated sensory organs; its discordance unnerves the 'apparent' concordance of his life under law. The thought of having been knocked down by a bazaar boy, to whom saving an animal (Maharani) is much more important, surprises Rusty's English sense of self-importance. It is too early for him to understand the existence or the validity of the pious practice of Hindus in which they worship cow as goddess. Even when Somi explains that his unintentional act of hurting Rusty is to avoid the wild cow, Rusty hardly believes him. This implies that Rusty is taking time to become accustomed to his new surroundings. Rusty's initial experience with real India is humiliating also because his vision matches the perspective of an outsider finding exoticism in an unfamiliar space. Rusty's immediate befuddlement at Somi's friendliness is then expected: 'His [Somi] laugh rang out merrily, and there was something about the laugh, some music in it perhaps, that touched a chord of gaiety in Rusty's own heart' (Bond 2010, 15). Somi's ringing laughter without malice during the bicycle ride is now revised as, 'Somi was smiling, and on his mouth the smile was friendly and in his soft brown eyes it was mocking' (15).

Dehra's bazaar, by its readiness to accept people across classes and communities, opposes the demarcated zone of the Europeans. It is here that Mr Harrison's English decorum is interrogated bluntly. The bazaar, in every possible way, shields against colonial ideology by enacting regional activities. If Rusty's trained Englishness boasts of colonial pretence, the bazaar advances a peripheral supremacy straightaway. What is more intriguing is that while his guardian transmits a sense of exclusivity in Rusty's young mind, the bazaar, displaying a sense of heterogeneous-togetherness, welcomes Rusty with its cosmopolitan appeal. Rusty's personal encounter with the harsh reality of the bazaar, thus, questions the 'self'. It is undeniable that Rusty's association with the larger India comes from a psychological necessity to emplace his 'self' outside his community's segregation so that an awareness of the truth of the mind can sprout. Rusty's escape, I argue, to the bazaar is, therefore, an escape from himself—the older self, conditioned and debilitated by Mr Harrison's strictures.

The narrative quickness to make Rusty dive into the bazaar terrain seems to come from the author-narrator's subjective inclination. Rusty's subsequent reading of this 'mysterious place' as a 'dream-bright world' reflects the narrator's desire to know the place, who was taught that the bazaar is a place replete with thieves and germs. Though the bazaar (which embodies the real India) is not physically far away, the people of his community refrain from talking about it. Overcoming this initial prejudice, Rusty now dreams of finding a home in it, where he evinces exasperation and finds a meaning of existence. Rusty's bazaar escapade frees him from his rigid lifestyle, unnerves John Harrison's autocratic worldview, and paves the way for the intersection of race-class discrepancy. It further enables the mixed-blood boy to see that he could start life afresh, without being a part of any colonial legacy.

From the very beginning, Rusty is impressed by Somi's carefree nature. In fact, Rusty is secretly charmed by Somi's persistence in helping a stranger in distress, which strengthens his faith and acts as an incentive in his internalising the bazaar. Considering Rusty's readiness in understanding a newcomer as a signifier to characteristic openness, Anglo-Indian scholar Bryan Peppin notes in his study:

> The first thing that strikes the reader about Rusty is that he is not inhibited. The reason for his initial aloofness is because he is not allowed beyond the confines of British India. This is all the more questionable because it is obvious that the story-line begins, in time, after Independence. The ride into the bazaar, on Somi's bicycle, is enough to cement a fast bond between the new-found friends. Plain talking by Somi makes Rusty realize the lop-sidedness of his "white-washed" world: Rusty rejects Somi's contention that he is a snob and promptly—to prove his point—joins him in the chaat shop. (2012, 26–27)

Rusty's camaraderie with Somi and his other Indian friends grants him a temporary relief from his guardian's rigidity. The early riding experience with Somi has underpinned the contrast between the life that he currently lives and a life that he might achieve. He was thrilled by the ride and solemnly curious to know the bazaar. To discover the bazaar means discovering India. Rusty is apprehensive yet exhilarated, susceptible yet happy. If the bicycle ride generates utmost sensation in Rusty's mind on the one side, it unfolds a new avenue for him outside the claustrophobic residue on the other:

> The wind hit them with a sudden force, and their clothes blew up like balloons, almost tearing them from the machine. The boy [Rusty] forgot his discomfort and clung desperately to the cross-bar, too nervous to say a word. Suri [Somi's friend] howled and Ranbir [Somi's another friend] kept telling him to shut up, but Somi was enjoying the ride. He laughed merrily, a clear, ringing laugh, a laugh that bore no malice and no derision but only enjoyment, fun . . . . (Bond 2010, 6)

Other than this exhilaration, the bicycle ride is a cathartic moment of revelation to him and can be viewed as an 'instrument for eradicating differences among people and restoring a sense of egalitarianism in society' (Bandyopadhyay 2012, 30). Had there been no accidental meeting and mutual exchange on the ride between Rusty and Somi, this friendship beyond racial differences might not have been so convincing. It is after his sudden confrontation with enthusiastic Somi, that Rusty notices 'Indians' carefully. Rusty's decision to discover the prohibited Indian bazaar with an intention to overcome the notion of disassociating Europeans from the 'natives' is laced with wonder. Therefore, the Indian bazaar he ventures past the Clock Tower may appear feverish and smelly at the first sight, but this is the world with confusion and contours that Rusty inwardly longs for:

> The boy plunged into the throng of bustling people; the road was hot and close, alive with the cries of vendors and the smell of cattle and ripening dung. Children played hopscotch in alleyways or gambled with coins, scuffling in the gutter for a lost anna. And the cows moved leisurely through the crowd, noising around for paper and stale, discarded vegetables; the more daring cows helping themselves at open stalls. And above the uneven tempo of the noise came the blare of a loudspeaker playing a popular piece of music. (Bond 2010, 13)

The bazaar association, in fact, disrupts his 'imposed' racial barrier. That is to say, the origin of Rusty's defiance is derived from his understanding, amidst the bazaar's democratic spirit, of the authoritarian force that curbs one's freedom. His preference to roam with Indian friends is indicative of his proclivity to pursue a life as an independent individual.

In the bazaar, Rusty's beyond-the-familiar-investigation is his tool to sense the seemingly indigestive world of affairs. But Rusty's self-transformative act of understanding the reality permits him to sensitise the bazaar's 'cohabitive' sphere. Carrying on with the bazaar's pervasive influence on him, Rusty's urge to defer his intimacy with this new space is to license the fictional process of self-making. His developing consciousness now concentrates on the imminent act of overcoming egocentricity and submission to the will that previously he could only dream of. The bazaar's complex dynamicity titillates him. Its haphazard state, where a multiplicity of thoughts commingles, is now reasoned by him. Rusty's conjoint investment of reason and dream makes the bazaar space a contact one, where one's thought is to be affected by other(s). With alteration of ideas comes reformation/reversal of one's destiny. The bazaar's inexhaustive sources of pleasures, which Rusty has observed in the course of action, also suggest multiple definitions of seeing life. Rusty seems to be impressed by the bazaar's extraordinary accommodative nature because his previous accommodation provided by his guardian is limited to singularity of thought. This at once complexifies and vivifies his belonging.

I have already suggested that the change of attitude of Rusty begins after his association with this bazaar culture. By unsettling his Western intellect awkwardly and unexpectedly, Somi interrogates his British snobbery; and by laughing out loud at finding Rusty in the gutter, he (Somi) wipes away the class division and power equation between them. Not surprisingly, when Somi extends his hand in the bazaar to help the white boy out of the gutter, Rusty tries to disregard the other's overtures. Although Rusty's inculcated self still tries to retain class superiority, Somi's behaviour prepares the former to appreciate friendliness. To prove that he is not a snob, Rusty joins the *chaat*-shop *adda*. The said *adda* (a Bengali word referring to an unrestricted, carefree gathering among friends or acquaintances, where anyone can express anything) enables Rusty to review that Somi's laughter essentially contains no sneer, no rigidity, no disregard, and no negligence. If anything, it communicates fellow-feeling.

Hence at the end of the *chaat*-shop *adda*, he accepts Somi's 'warm muddy hand' (Bond 2010, 16) overcoming his ego. Somi's carefree laughter, instead of irritating him, now takes Rusty to the point of passive submission to the former's wishes. By generating a limitless zone, this *adda* makes passage to the depth of local culture through street foods. *Tikkee* (fried potato cake), in the meantime, replaces lemonade in Rusty's terrain. Along with *tikkee*, he also relishes the cultural depth and variety of India. Lemonade in a proper container is no longer a requisite, and it is supplanted now by multi-layered and sensational street-foods on plain leaves. Somi has this to say: 'After tikkees you must have something else, *chaat* or *golguppas*, all right?' (17). Somi's spontaneity in preparing the boy for these foods as compared to the orderly preparations of the missionary's wife is the textual explanation of desired relief from the bracketed life on the part of the author's alter-ego. Rusty's endeavour to sit cross-legged on the ground in the *chaat*-shop (in the Indian style) formulates and refers to Buddha's meditation, an epiphany to have a clearer vision about life so far disregarded.

The *chaat-adda* serves two aspects: By joining the *adda*, Rusty dissents his community's unwritten law; while by including Rusty in it, the *adda* helps him see life inside the bazaar. It constitutes a contact zone not merely between, for example, Rusty and Somi but between the two worlds they represent. *Adda*, one of the unique and inventive forms of gossip, generates a carefree space, where its participants express their heart out. *Adda* precipitates neither restriction nor compulsion. It does not force to conform to a point of disagreement. If there is anything other than Holi, the Indian spring festival, at this juncture of *The Room* to provide the right environment to exchange mutual understanding, it is this informal and unrigorous *chaat*-shop congregation. Moreover, if *adda* carries the older sense of dwelling or gathering place, Rusty feels at ease among his friends. He enjoys their easy acceptance and feels more inclined towards their company. It is through this *adda* that Rusty attains a group identity (even when each of them is different in terms of religion, caste or upbringing; they are all Indian), which is further articulated in the Holi celebration. The reference of *adda* is also significant because it simultaneously holds cultural purity and cultural plurality. In it, Rusty and Somi's lifestyles contradict as well as comingle.

Theoretically, *adda* also suggests many voices, or what Mikhail Bakhtin terms 'heteroglossia', in which anyone can establish his voice. In her article 'Speech Genres and Identity', Debarati Sen interestingly puts: 'I would not say that *adda* was a resistance to westernization, it was not a conscious attempt by the Bengali middle class to use it as a medium of subversion, but its effects point towards a process of hybridization of modes of expression' (2011, 526). Be as it may, but the role of *adda* as an agency of questioning, subversion and diversity is tenable. The bazaar's *chaat*-shop, where the *adda* takes place, is an all-new world for Rusty. It is here that he watches the art of making spicy *tikkees*, is surprised at and learns Somi's cross-legged sitting, tastes hot and spicy food on banana leaf, and experiences hospitality from his Indian friends. Even after he learns that oily *tikkee* might cause stomach upset, he feels no displeasure to consume it. Behind Rusty's immediate befuddled reaction after the gutter experience works a subconscious process of assessing his position and measuring the carefree laughter of Somi, his would-be 'best favourite friend' in a short while. Which is why, at the end of the first *chaat-adda*, when Somi extends his welcoming hand, Rusty fails to deny it. While shaking Somi's dirty hand Rusty reviews his ego and leaves a passage open for friendship to be stapled during successive events. If crossing the Clock Tower is the first key step to witness a culturally variant Indian life, Rusty's active participation, after little hesitancy, in the Indian carnival of Holi helps him experience its depth. By participating in it, Rusty erases the remaining fear of being disloyal and goes beyond the dialectic of race and class.

Meanwhile, one can hardly deny that the bazaar *adda*, replacing his withdrawn attitude, infuses in Rusty an unoccupied spirit. In the following meeting, therefore, when Somi sympathises with Rusty, '[b]y what misfortune are you an Englishman?[4] How is it that you have been here all your life and never been to a *chaat* shop before?' (Bond 2010, 17), the latter discloses his discomfit at his guardian's strict upbringing. While Somi and his friends guide Rusty to show the wider world, Dehra's bazaar helps him experience it. If *chaat*-shop *adda* with *tikkee*, *chaat* (a spicy mixture of salad made of potato, orange and guava) and *golguppa* (a flour-made round, crisp and hollow snack served with spicy water or pickle) brings new flavours in his life, his active participation in Holi makes him recognise his repressed present. In defiance of his guardian's order, the boy now accepts Ranbir's invitation to play Holi with Dehra's bazaar boys.Holi, attributing a symbolic connotation of awakening, clarifies Rusty's doubts underpinning that there should be no demarcation between 'them' and 'us'; 'black' and 'white'; 'English' and 'native'; at least among those who live in the country. Once he participates in this Indian spring festival, his ego is erased thoroughly, enabling him to go beyond the binaries of proper and improper, decent and indecent, superior and inferior:

> For one day, Ranbir and his friends forgot their homes and their work and the problem of the next meal, and danced down the roads, out of the town and into the forest. And, for one day, Rusty forgot his guardian and the missionary's wife and the supple malacca cane, and ran with the others through the town and into the forest. (26)

On the surface, Holi revives his consciousness that the privileged hierarchy and racial myth of John Harrison will eventually dampen his individuation; on a deeper level, it outdoes Rusty's English (imposed) decency by successfully instilling Indian cultural nuances. His pains are replaced with pleasures now. He becomes one of the bazaar boys. They are his reality henceforth. If Holi makes its participants forget about their daily hardships and poverty, it is on the same occasion that Rusty forgets 'his guardian and the missionary's wife and the supple malacca cane' (26) and feel 'another world' in which the pain of his body becomes 'a pleasure' (27). Rusty's active immersion into the game is significant as it reconfirms the novelist's desire for human contact.

Rusty has repeatedly been warned to keep a safe distance from the bazaar lest his English decency be tainted. But, on the day of Holi, the insistent drum beats reminds Rusty of his promise of playing the game and finding an opportunity to closely follow his new interest. Ranbir's *dholak*, as a token of welcome, conjoins with the rhythms and excitement of the countless drums of the bazaar and incites Rusty to leave his residue to join the dream-reality that might correlate his dream of becoming impulsive and wild and propel him to materialise the dream of 'thrashing Mr Harrison until the guardian begged for mercy' (Bond 2010, 22). From the guardian's perspective, once he crosses the terrain and participates in the festival of sharing love, he loses his European identity: 'How can you call yourself an Englishman, how can you come back to this house in such a condition? In what gutter, in what brothel have you been! Have you seen yourself? Do you know what you look like?' (28). Mr Harrison's disparaging comments, in turn, compels Rusty to consider a life outside his influence.

By engaging himself in Holi, in which people from varied strata actively take part and sense newness of life, Rusty not merely revises his existence but dethrones his community's imaginary barrier. Under this spring carnival, he sensitises a mystical union with diversifying Indian life. Rusty's English education collapses before the Indian festival of colour and results in a disparaging rubric of 'wild, ragged, ungrateful wretch' from his guardian (Bond 2010, 27). His English decency is replaced with the metaphoric 'filth' (28) that Holi imparts. If Rusty's move from his guardian's English residence towards the throbbing practicality of the bazaar directs him to gather real-life experiences on the one side, his involvement in Holi manumits himself on the other. He knows that on the other side of the Clock Tower rests life.

On being challenged by the boy, Mr John Harrison receives a tremendous shock:

> He felt a wave of anger, and then a wave of pain: was this the boy he had trained and educated—this wild, ragged, ungrateful wretch, who did not know the difference between what was proper and what was improper, what was civilized and what was barbaric, what was decent and what was shameful—and had the years of training come to nothing? (27–28)

The act of upending his values by his ward is beyond his imagination, and hence his rage has no limit. Forgetting his politicised origin, Mr Harrison's infuriated sneer at Rusty indirectly questions his own status as being a 'half-caste'. Mr Harrison is a flat uni-dimensional character in this novel and he remains undeveloped throughout by keeping hold of his opinions; as he compares Rusty to a 'mongrel' (28) maintaining his English hierarchical veneer, his disregard, in turn, critiques his own predicament, when Rusty is no longer behaving like a European: 'I'm no better than the sweeper boy, but I'm as good and him! I'm as good as you! I'm as good as anyone!' (29).

In a 'carnivalistic' world, Mikhail Bakht in writes in *Problems of Dostoevsky's Poetics*, 'what is suspended first of all is hierarchical structure and all the forms of terror, reverence, piety, and etiquette connected with it—that is, everything resulting from socio-hierarchical inequality or any other form of inequality among people' (1984, 123). A direct instance of hierarchical subversion, levelling and degradation occur when Rusty, enraged at Mr Harrison's cruelty, pays him back: 'Rusty gripped him by the collar and pushed him backwards until they both fell over on to the floor. With one hand still twisting the collar, the boy slapped his guardian's face' (Bond 2010, 29). He is not the same docile boy with an appeased attitude anymore, but a revived identity who dares to emerge into manhood from the safe centre of his guardian:

> Mad with the pain in his own face, Rusty hit the man again and again, wildly and awkwardly, but the giddy thrill of knowing he could do it: he was a child no longer, he was nearly seventeen, he was a man. He could inflict pain, that was a wonderful discovery; there was a power in his body—a devil or a god—and he gained confidence in his power; and he was a man! (29)

Rusty's slap may apparently be a reactionary act of Mr Harrison's physical torture, but it undermines the latter's guardianship and officialdom. Mr Harrison's utterance of the word 'mongrel'—a disrespectful term suggesting one's half-Indian-half-British stature—is a result of surprise. In later episodes, Rusty's frequent hints at considering himself a 'mongrel' are basically to ridicule Mr Harrison's inability to understand the poignancy of the expression. Rusty's slap also curbs Mr Harrison's colonial authority in the literary sense and implicitly strikes back the British political agenda that once accompanied the emergence of the mixed-blood race and their consequent dilemma. The Rusty-John Harrison contestation not only mandates the former's reaction to the physical punishment but also retaliates Mr Harrison's autocratic position. The slap as peripheral supremacy over Mr Harrison's centralised and ruling position is meaningfully similar to the previous dismantling of the ruler-ruled order by means of the *tikkee*-lemonade conflict.

Resistance in *The Room* is predominantly acted out through different modes of opposition and subversion and is represented in dissimilar activities at both ends, which mostly revolve around the bazaar. Mr Harrison's decision to lead an isolated life to resist indigenisation cannot be reasoned, at least to Rusty's self-transformative liberal consciousness, in post-independent India. For, once Rusty walks into the Indian bazaar and associates with

Somi and his friends against his guardian's will, the very process of associating with everything Indian commences. The guardian-ward contention, in this regard, is notable because a member of the Anglo-Indian community is, in this book, employed to expose and defy the ideology of another member of the same community. Mr Harrison's lashing sneer towards Rusty can also be interpreted as a discursive mechanism to ridicule his own 'privileged' position. This contestation, however, opens up two important issues: first, it articulates a tendency of the Anglo-Indians either to dissolve into the Indian mainstream or to hold their racial distinctiveness in the post-independent phase; and second, it entails that Rusty, despite having a mixed lineage, perceives his reality merely as an Indian beyond racial identification. This directs us to consider Mr John Harrison's racial superiority from a more liberal point of view and not from avantage point of the Anglo-Indians who desire to lead a segregated life outside the orbit of Dehra's bazaar.

Escape to Emerge: Exclusivity to Individuation

> [O]f all the many elephant traps lying ahead of us, the largest and most dangerous pitfall would be the adoption of a ghetto mentality. To forget that there is a world beyond the community to which we belong, to confine ourselves within narrowly defined cultural frontiers, would be, I believe, to go voluntarily into that form of internal exile [...]. (Rushdie 2010, 19)

Salman Rushdie's formulation of the 'ghetto mentality' hinders development of the self. Its harrowing effect leading one into self-exile is already experienced by the authorial identity in Britain. In his memoir *Scenes*, Ruskin Bond, at the time of his departure from his stepfather's house in pursuit of personal space, stresses: 'I was the angry young man [at the age of sixteen], in revolt against rules, traditions, conventions, examinations, authority of any kind'

(2012, 323). In a similar vein, Rusty, the author's contextualist sense of being, revolts against his guardian and leaves the address behind. After drifting away completely from Mr Harrison's sphere of influence, Rusty sensitises the zeal of a free identity, despite the fact that he will have to spend a night under Dehra's open sky until Somi takes him home next day. As Rusty closes the chapter of Mr Harrison, he is now free from caning. Yet, mental colonisation that once had shaped him continues to tease his self; the rest of the novel bears testimony of this battle as a constant intervention so as to reformulate his 'once' slanted identity. His individual quest for identity—'who am I?'—may contradict the dogma of his community, but in the long run, it complements his endeavour to reinforce his tie with his nation. Talking about the novel's criteria as a bildungsroman, Bond's biographer Meena Khorana sums up:

> Poised at a turning point in his life, Rusty is ready for a dynamic confrontation with Indian culture. As the hero of an archetypal journey would do, Rusty responds to the "call to adventure" and crosses into forbidden realms, where he faces many challenges on the road to adulthood and independence. (2003, 31)

We must not forget that Rusty's initial curiosity to venture past the Clock Tower into the bazaar was not merely to satiate an adolescent's adventure-prone mind but to necessitate the authorial self's insistence to get rid of social isolation. With breaking away from the Anglo-Indian backdrop, he enters the throbbing practicality of India: 'This act of "crossing the threshold",' Khorana writes, 'symbolizes his psychological need to empower himself, and his readiness to take responsibility for his life and actions. He returns to the bazaar, the very womb of life, and is born anew' (2003, 33). Seen thus, *The Room* is a story of the protagonist's struggle for personal autonomy beneath an apparent journey of finding true domesticity of a school-pass-out-vagabond. In the bazaar, Rusty also finds a teaching job, and with this he manages a room of his own. The geometrically small (with a string bed, table, and a shelf) but spatially wide room on the roof of the Kapoor family comes with hope, sustenance and liberty. The room with a window entails privacy and insight and serves as a site for self-making. The assurance and comfort of the room are better felt with familial support and playmates. The open heartedness of his bazaar friends makes him more inclined towards them. Rusty's understanding that love knows only love and it is complemented by mutual sharing comes from his gradual association with Dehra's bazaar culture. This is because, the European identity in Rusty starts transforming within, and hence the taboo of Dehra's bazaar is now replaced with a world of conviction to construe reality.

Rusty's initial angst is to license him a free space outside the static existence, largely weighed down by monolithic world views. Rusty's act of defying his English education not only argues against his guardian but intervenes in his so-long ghettoised self. The idea of his Anglicised self is questioned in the clash between the free-bazaar zone and social isolation of his community. If this encounter ascertains his repressed lifestyle and deepens his vexation, this, in turn, erases the deterrent for the betterment of the individual. Rusty's in competence to lead a life ignoring his background, as his Indian friends was not initially realised because of a sense of moral obligation towards his guardian. He now cannot be someone unlike Somi or Ranbir because his 'half-caste' identity essentially makes no sense to him. Earlier, when Mr Harrison rebukes him by questioning his origin, Rusty is disturbed by his delimiting rhetoric. Rusty's defiance to outwit his guardian's imposed theory now allows him to move away from his community's insularity towards individual call. That is to say, Rusty's fraternising with Somi and others registers positive furtherance from narrowness to enlightenment, class consciousness to togetherness, and, above all, from the prejudiced mindset to a secular terrain. One might, however, presume an altogether different outcome, had Rusty got a better guardian.

In a novel replete with elaborate descriptions of identity-formation, the novelist introduces varied ifs and thens before his central character to test his temperament. Rusty's failure to decode any substantive difference in terms of skin-colour in Suri (a Kashmiri) until Kishen highlights the dissimilarity, or his inattention to invest much in Somi's 'golden brown' skin, is a personal import from the author-narrator's disinterest in race and *varna*. Presumably because, Bond is particularly interested in Rusty, an adolescent who happened to be an Anglo-Indian, but not in Anglo-Indian theme. Naturally, finding oneness in heterogeneity is what the text suggests. Therefore, the novelist's vision of blending two oppositional forces as a unified whole in Rusty, stands out prominently. While foregrounding the complexity of postcolonial condition with reference to Rusty, Roderick McGillis's observation in his entry 'Postcolonialism: Originating Difference' is worthwhile:

> Individual finds themselves inextricably caught up in political and cultural forces. The boy in the story, and Bond himself, know no other country as home but India; in reality, Ruskin Bond did not go away; he continues to live in India and to write about that country. He is well known in India as an Indian writer, but he is a member of a diasporic group, connected through family history and education to a non-Indian past, to a past and a country that played the colonizer to the colonized India. In this period of post-independence in India, where does a writer like Ruskin Bond fit in? (2004, 893)

Besides concentrating on the quest motif, which recurs in the narrative, this discussion seeks to step in and figure out the debate that McGillis raises in the case of Rusty, the counterpart of the author who 'grew up as an Indian with no division of loyalties, but as the inheritor of a dual culture' (Khorana 1995, 253). *The Room* registers the struggle of meaning-making in life experienced by Anglo-Indian Rusty, who, is born in colonial India and brought up in the 1940s, and is a subject of critical attention. If there is a sense of dilemma in Rusty's mind due to his multi-racial past, it is further developed in post-independent India. McGillis rightly detects the predicament of this

Anglo-Indian boy but overlooks Rusty's inclination in so far as Rusty's journey corroborates a substantive move from (quasi)-Englishness to Indianness, which also lends an inner-voyage. There is a suggestion, as indicated earlier, that by letting Rusty cross the margin of colonial prejudice of Mr Harrison and embrace India's diverse genetic mix, the authorial-self encases a journey within. A close consideration also assures that Rusty's journey to Haridwar (spelt as Hardwar in the text) entails the author's physical journey to England. Interestingly, there is no such journey outside India undertaken by Bond's fictional self in this text; the novelist restricts his protagonist within the national geography to clarify that the true home for Rusty resides in the diverse world of India.

Restriction, snobbery and aloofness are malefactors that make Rusty dispirited. As against the kind, accommodating Somi, Mr Harrison's house is a vicious sphere, which fades away once he rubs shoulders with Dehra's boys. Their relationship is as if what distresses the boy delights the guardian and vice versa. It becomes clearer when his reticent guardian is juxtaposed with Somi and his abode with the *chaat* shop. Mr Harrison's indifference to Rusty is counterbalanced by Somi's compassion. Rusty is aware of the commonality that he has with the Indian boy. There is, however, no conscious endeavour on Rusty's part to connect with his other Indian friends. Textual references suggest that it happens almost instinctively, based on that commonality and sentiment. In *A Passage to India*, E.M. Forster proposes a connection through Dr Aziz but fails to give any assurance. The depth of the Rusty-Somi camaraderie, however, brings forth the oft-lost conviction found in many narratives dealing with East-West encounters. An understanding that Somi or any of his friends never disassociates Rusty either by disparaging his whiteness or treating him as 'other' is achieved. If his community is too concerned to retain mythos in isolating themselves from the rest of India, Dehra shows him an unfettered life outside the rigidities of *varna*. This self-awareness individuates Rusty from the other members of his community; he can associate with the bazaar because he feels the essence of it. He feels that it too has life—a life full of contours and vividness, hardship and endurance—but life nonetheless. Rusty's experience of the bazaar reality promulgates the idea that being an Indian also means acknowledging one's communal existence.

Rusty's reliance on his Indian friends, however, sours when they start leaving Dehra one after another. Overwhelmed at Kishen's departure, Rusty's heart cries out: 'Inside of me,' he said, 'I am all lonely . . .' (Bond 2010, 86). Now, even the privacy and self-reliance of his room on the roof at Kapoor's terrace gives him no solace. It must be admitted that although Rusty undergoes a deep sense of solitariness in absence of his friends, there is no sense of exile on his part. Of course, the 'half-caste' stigma triggered by his *métis* origin resounds to affect his adolescent mind. He thus discloses his pain agonisingly, in the process of self-evaluation, to his 'best favourite friend': 'But I don't belong here, Somi. I don't belong anywhere. Even if I have papers, I don't belong. I'm a half-caste, I know it, and that is as good as not belonging anywhere' (90).

Rusty's decision of leaving Dehra is, however, withdrawn at the end of the novel. For, once he meets Kishen—his one-time student, playmate and brother—he soon feels alive. At their reunion in Haridwar, Rusty realises that they are 'each other's refuge' (Bond 2010, 113) and his tie with India is deeply foregrounded: 'He could not run away. He could not escape the life he had made, the ocean into which he had floundered the night he left his guardian's house. He had to return to the room; *his* room; he had to go back' (113). Rusty's elderly care for Kishen seems to replicate a relationship where the multi-racial father adopts an Indian son, thus completing his emotional conversation to Indianness.

While discussing postcolonial autobiography, C.L. Innes argues that '[t]hinking about these autobiographical works, one is struck by how often travel, the move away from a starting place, becomes in postcolonial autobiography a means of locating oneself back in that land' (2007, 70). Bond's memoir *Scenes*, I have discussed in the preceding chapter, narrates the journey of the authorial self from India to the UK to review his true origin. Concurrently in *The Room*, Rusty's move from Dehra to Haridwar suggests his rootedness to Dehra's sensory evocation of the place. In Haridwar, when Rusty dips in the holy Ganges, his relationship with his native place finds a definite articulation. With this, he is secularised into an Indian life and builds an eternal bond with his motherland:

> Lying on his belly on the riverbank, he drank of the holy waters. Then he pulled off his shirt and sandals and slipped into the water. There were men and women on all sides, praying with their faces to the sun. Great fish swam around them, unafraid and unmolested, safe in the sacred waters of the Ganges. (Bond 2010, 108)

The novel does not end here because the author-narrator further necessitates a strong root for Rusty in India, ignoring his white race. Accompanied by Kishen, he returns to Dehra's warmth to solidify his 'tie' and to be accepted by the Indian cultural fabric. The author enunciates: 'His return was justified' (113). The reference to Dehra as a site of return has re-emerged as a space of enlightenment to Rusty. One cannot altogether deny that Rusty's inner-contradiction is now not between to be an Indian and not to be an Indian. Rather, his return to Dehra means returning to the self, to the personal history not burdened by cultural and historical obscurity but with an endless self-questioning and promise.

The novelist's choice of Haridwar as the connecting place between Rusty and Kishen is also significant. As a Hindu pilgrimage site, it is perhaps assumed that the town spiritually boosts positivity among its pilgrims. Rusty, while roaming the Ganges ghats, finds the essence of life by witnessing humane significances amidst varied ritualistic practices of the worshippers. The complete attention to the Hindu ritual associated with the Ganges on the part of an Anglo-Indian symbolises a preference for the Indian culture to an English one. Rusty's heartfelt dip, therefore, in the water of the holy Ganges does not merely connote his baptism, but also acts to censor the tendentious English instructions of his guardian. By reinforcing a complete disregard of austerity, it renders togetherness. We are directed to think that Rusty's dip is a symbolic washing away of all vestigial prejudices, following an initiation to the Indian ethos. On the boat in Haridwar (literally, the gateway to God), Rusty's voyage of self-discovery is accentuated by an old woman's curiosity: 'What are you my son, are you one of us? I have never, on the river, seen blue eyes and golden hair' (Bond 2010, 112). The pilgrim's doubt in accepting Rusty as an Indian revises Somi's inquisitiveness in the initial pages: 'A European boy was no longer a common sight in Dehra' (4). Rusty's defence of self-hood, affected by and achieved after ritualistic purification with a keen understanding, is something by which he could belong anywhere and everywhere, and that his identity cannot be judged only by his ordained ethnicity. Even though Rusty encounters questions about his mixed-blood status, he is free to evince that an Anglo-Indian is also an Indian, and that race can hardly dissemble one's nationality. National and religious identification appear stronger than racial identification to Rusty, and therefore his quest for individual choice seems fulfilling at the end. If *The Room* is an articulation of an Anglo-Indian identity travelling from communal exclusivity towards individuation, it also denotes a journey taken by Rusty from seclusion to inclusion.

Notes

1. When *The Room* was first published by Andre Deutsch, it was described as 'an adult novel written by a teenager'. In 1957, it won The *John Llewellyn Rhys Memorial Prize*, the second oldest literary award in Britain, which was annually offered to the 'most memorable work of any kind' by an author who is under thirty. For more, see Prabhat K. Singh cited below.
2. Mr Harrison's abode does not render the intimacy of a *ghar* or *bari* (alternatively stands for home) to Rusty. Because the idea of *ghar*/*bari* connotes a very personal space lost in Harrison's rigidness.

3. Here, Dehra suggests the European corner where Rusty lives with his guardian.
4. It is expected that as a colonial practice and to camouflage the inferiority complex associated with their community, Mr Harrison is purposefully ignorant about the Anglo-Indian racial-mix. In the text, Somi too generalises Rusty's complex belongingness. What is, however, evident is that he seems to have Rusty's quasi-Englishness in mind.

Bibliography

Anthony, Frank. 1969. *Britain's Betrayal in India: The Story of the Anglo-Indian Community*. New Delhi: Allied Publishers.

Ashcroft, Bill. 2001. *Post-Colonial Transformation*. London, UK: Routledge.

Boehmer, Elleke. 2005. *Colonial and Postcolonial Literature: Migrant Metaphors*. New Delhi: Oxford University Press.

Bakhtin, M.M. 1984. *Problems of Dostoevsky's Poetics*, ed. and trans. Caryl Emerson. Minnesota: University of Minnesota Press.

Bandyopadhyay, Debashis. 2012. *Locating the Anglo-Indian Self in Ruskin Bond: A Postcolonial Review*. New Delhi: Anthem.

Bond, Ruskin. 2010. 'The Room on the Roof'. *Classic Ruskin Bond Vol. 1: The Novels*. New Delhi: Penguin, 1–114.

———. 2012. 'Scenes from a Writer's Life'. *Classic Ruskin Bond Vol. 2: The Memoirs*. New Delhi: Penguin.

———. 2016. *Room on the Roof: 60th Anniversary Edition*. New Delhi: Penguin.

Caplan, Lionel. 2001. *Children of Colonialism: Anglo-Indians in a Postcolonial World*. Oxford: Berg.

D'Costa, A. 2006. 'Anglo-Indian Nostalgia: Longing for India as Homeland', *Second Annual Rhizomes: Re-visioning Boundaries Conference of The School of Languages and Comparative Cultural Studies*, February, Brisbane, Australia. Unpublished conference paper. The University of Queensland, 1–11. Available at: https://espace.library.uq.edu.au/view/UQ:7724/adc_rhiz.pdf (accessed on 13 February 2016).

Innes, C.L. 2007. *The Cambridge Introduction to Postcolonial Literatures in English*. New York: Cambridge University Press.

Khorana, Meena G. 1995. 'The River Is Eternal: Nature Mysticism and Vedanta Philosophy in Ruskin Bond's Angry River', *The Lion and the Unicorn* 19(2): 253–68.

Khorana, Meena G. 2003. *The Life and Works of Ruskin Bond*. Westport, CT: Praeger.

McGillis, Roderick. 2004. 'Postcolonialism: Originating Difference'. In *International Companion Encyclopedia of Children's Literature: Volume I*, edited by Peter Hunt, 2nd ed. London: Routledge, 891–900. *Google Book Search*. 4 January 2016.

Peppin, Bryan. 2012. *Black and White: The "Anglo-Indian" Identity in Recent English Fiction*. Central Milton Keynes, UK: Author House.

Rushdie, Salman. 2010. *Imaginary Homelands: Essays and Criticism 1981–1991*. London: Vintage.

Said, Edward W. 1994. *Culture and Imperialism*. London: Vintage.

Sen, Debarati. 2011. 'Speech Genres and Identity: The Place of *Adda* in Bengali Cultural Discourse', *Journal of Emerging Knowledge on Emerging Markets*, 3 (November): 521–34. Available at: Citeseerx (accessed on 15 May 2016).

Singh, Prabhat K., ed. 1995. *The Creative Contours of Ruskin Bond: An Anthology of Critical Writings*. New Delhi: Pencraft.

Tiffin, Helen. 1995. 'Post-colonial Literatures and Counter-discourse'. In *The Post-Colonial Studies Reader*, edited by B. Ashcroft, G. Griffiths and H. Tiffin. London: Routledge, 95–98.

4

Liberating Motherhood

Mariam Labadoor in *A Flight of Pigeons*

In *The Room on the Roof*, Rusty's act of emancipating himself from the ghettoised existence of Dehra's European order does not, however, reinstate altogether disregard of his double-inheritance. The book entails a sequential progress of self-making legitimised through Mariam's socialising with an unprejudiced mindset in *A Flight of Pigeons* (henceforth *A Flight*). From the 'secluded European section' of Dehra, the narratorial-self now shifts to a 'small English community' of Shahjahanpur. This underpinned evolvement suggests a change of perspective from being an outside (and somewhat confused) voice to an inside one. Expectedly, the idea of seclusion is withdrawn in the text conceptualised about twenty years after the inception of *The Room*. Moreover, in terms of physical appearance of the hero-narrator, Rusty's 'blue eyes and fair hair' are altered to the 'raven black hair and dark eyes' of Ruth, the narrator of *A Flight*. Also, while the boy-hero of *The Room* had to overcome moral obligations and communal disagreement in mixing with the other Indians and low-caste people, in *A Flight*, Mariam, Ruth's mother, participates in public gossips with her 'Indian' servants without any moral restrains. One may delimit Mariam's mingling as an exception, but this seems to be the novelist's key intention, i.e., essentialising the Anglo-Indian individuality.

Set against the backdrop of the 1857 Mutiny, Ruskin Bond's *A Flight of Pigeons* (serialised in *The Illustrated Weekly of India* in 1975) insists that it is not necessarily true that an Anglo-Indian (erstwhile Eurasian) woman is prejudiced against other Indian 'natives'.[1] Mariam Labadoor, the centre of our discussion, is an Anglo-Indian, who maintains an easy relationship both with her 'Indian' neighbours as well as with her European ones. Mariam, despite her Christian upbringing, is well aware of Muslim values, which even some Muslims of Shahjahanpur are unaware of. From the very beginning of the text, we note her ability to read the agitating situation and her alacrity to respond to the politically stirred-up atmosphere. Here, I shall focus on whether the representation of Mariam debunks stereotypes associated with the Anglo-Indian woman identity. Before we closely follow Mariam in the narrative, we shall briefly consider how Bond's interest is mingled with one of the greatest human events in Indian history—a fact which affirms that '[n]ot political history but the history of places and ordinary people engages Bond' (Kohli 2005, 132).

It is discernable that Bond's creative effort in the novel surpasses the mere limitation of historiography by directing it as a tale of endurance and mutual respect in the context of the Sepoy Mutiny. The narrative is set in Shahjahanpur, a small north-Indian town of Uttar Pradesh located about 250 miles away from Delhi. Besides the fact that his father, Aubrey Bond, was born in the Shahjahanpur military camp, Bond's firsthand experience of the town, where he visited sometime in the 1960s, perhaps intrigued him more in turning the history of this place into a story of human bravery. Other than historical authenticity, Bond's choice of Shahjahanpur as setting lies in his personal philosophy, too, of conceptualising India in small towns. If one looks back on Bond's personal life, he realises how well-knit his connection is with the privacy of small places, where life is self-reliant and uncomplicated. The novelist's intention here, we understand, is not to detail the kaleidoscopic milieu of this particular locale to deviate the narrative from its motive, but to manifest a shed of life and its involvement in situational crisis revolving around an Anglo-Indian Labadoor family.

In the late 1960s, when Ruskin Bond's success as a writer was still an event in the future, he switched to reading Indian history, with a particular interest in Anglo-Indian life in the Indian subcontinent. In his preface to *Strange Men Strange Places*, first published in 1969, he humorously notes:

> Professional historians will, I hope, forgive this intrusion into their domain by a mere story-teller. But so little has been written in recent times about those odd, colourful (and admittedly not very 'great') soldiers of fortune—mostly European—who strutted across the Indian subcontinent during the eighteenth and nineteenth centuries, that I felt a sort of compulsion to resurrect and retell some of their more glorious (or inglorious) exploits—not so much because their lives throw some light on the times they lived in, and help us to understand manners, morals and values of Europeans and Asians during a period of colonial expansion. (xi)

Bond went through numerous historical collections during this period.[2] The books of his interest that deserve special mention are: William Franklin's *The Military Memories of James Skinner* (1851), H.G. Keene's *Hindustan under the Free Lances* (1907), Mrs Eliza Fay's *The Original Letters from India* (1908), E.F. Oaten's *European Travellers in India, 1400–1700* (1909), Arnold Wright's *Early English Adventurers in India* (1917) and Douglas Dewar's *In the Days of the Company* (1920). It was at this point, that he was attracted to a diary entitled *Mariam: A Story of the Indian Mutiny of 1857* (1896) by J.F. Fanthome, which recounts the experiences of an Anglo-Indian girl named Ruth. Bond's decision to recreate Fanthome's narrative from a rigid historical reading as an interracial and interreligious commentary of goodness in a vexed time, suggests his desire to read the event on a humanitarian premise. Thus in *A Flight*, the reader encounters how an Anglo-Indian family is helped by Hindus, Muslims and Sikhs when they are at the mercy of mutineers. It is also implied that the novelist's act of telling Mariam's story comes from, what Meenakshi Mukherjee finds a fresh interest among Indian authors in the late 19th century, 'the desire to rewrite these accounts from an indigenous point of view' (1985, 40). Interestingly yet relevantly, Ruskin Bond's inclination towards the mid/late-19th-century history, we presume from his autobiographical references, seems to have emerged both from his intimacy with Victorian literature and an identity solidifying process. Born in the colonial period with a racially mixed baggage, Bond's interest in history, specifically in the 1857 human event, perhaps incited him to concentrate on racial interactions and render a plausible interpretation for them.

On a deeper investigation, it is revealed that Ruskin Bond is obsessed with presenting 'life' in fiction; hence, perhaps, the inclusion of 'Prologue' in the text. Apart from a novelistic experiment, it prefaces important information as background reading from where one can gauge the charged-up scenario of Uttar Pradesh, the imminent danger for the 'innocent' Europeans, and Mariam's extraordinary readiness to prepare for the unavoidable catastrophe. When she learns about agitated Meerut, a north-Indian town in the state of Uttar Pradesh, Mariam predicts something menacing will immediately affect the lives of the whites in Shahjahanpur and therefore she warns her husband and daughter to disassociate themselves from certain meetings. The negligence of her warning results in the tragic demise of her husband by enraged mutineers. With this politically charged backdrop in mind, Bond shows authorial reticence by making 14-year-old Ruth, the eyewitness, as his voice. In the 'Notes', the novelist informs us:

> I first heard the story of Mariam and her daughter from my father, who was born in the Shahjahanpur military cantonment a few years after the Mutiny. That, and my interest in the accounts of those who had survived the 1857 uprising, took me to Shahjahanpur on a brief visit in the late 1960s. It was one of those small UP towns that had resisted change, and there were no high-rise buildings or blocks of flats to stifle the atmosphere. I found the old church of St. Mary's without any difficulty, and beside it is a memorial to those who were killed there on that fateful day. It was surrounded by a large, open parade ground, bordered by mango groves and a few old bungalows. It couldn't have been very different in Ruth Labadoor's time. The little River Khannaut was still crossed by a bridge of boats. (2010, 370)

The Labadoor family consists of Mr Labadoor, a Frenchman of 42, Mariam Labadoor, a social, steady and concerned housewife, and their daughter Ruth Labadoor. A brief family history of Mariam from her maternal side would help us understanding her roots and the present discussion:

> Mrs. Labadoor's father had been a French adventurer who had served in the Maratha army; her mother came from a well-known Muslim family of Rampur. Her name was Mariam. She and her brothers had been brought up as Christians. At eighteen, she married Labadoor, a quiet, unassuming man, who was a clerk in the magistrate's office. He was the grandson of a merchant from Jersey (in the Channel Islands), and his original Jersey name was Labadu. (Bond 2010, 291)

Lionel Caplan has reminded us that we should not be surprised at such Euro-Indian unions, which were fairly common during the time (2010, 865). The story begins when Ruth, accompanied by her father, attends the usual Sunday prayer at St. Mary's disregarding her mother's premonition:

> Father and I had just left the house when we saw several sepoys crossing the road, on their way to the river for their morning bath. They stared so fiercely at us that I pressed close to my father and whispered, "Papa, how strange they look!". (Bond 2010, 293)

One should, at this juncture, know that during the second half of the 19th century, Shahjahanpur witnessed quite a large number of Afghan Pathans presumably commissioned by Bahadur Shah Zafar,[3] the then Mughal emperor. The British had already opted for Shahjahanpur as one of their cantonments. The clash was imminent. As hinted earlier, there was considerable tension between the British and the Indian 'natives' in the town. Whereas the local Indians lived together despite religious or caste conflicts, the town's European residents mostly remained separated and detached. The sole exception, in the text, is Mrs Labadoor. The *sepoys* are, however, so infuriated with the *angrez* that they do not refrain from slaughtering them even when church service is in progress. The Labadoor house, like many *firangi* abodes, is set on fire leaving its members nowhere to go. They somehow hide in a nearby mud house until Lala Ramjimal, a local Kayastha, rescues them to his house. The textual information is supported by factual evidence given in the introduction to *The Penguin 1857 Reader*:

> The telegraph wires were cut and there was no way the Meerut officers could contact other regiments for help. Looting and plunder proceeded briskly. Englishmen's bungalows were burnt and many killed with their families. Some sepoys and native servants, however, helped their English officers and their families to escape at great risk to themselves. (Nayar 2007, 10)

The suppressed outbursts of the *sepoys* also stress how the novelist implicitly questions the trope of the mindset that views the Great Indian Uprising as a revolt of the oppressive kind. The *sepoys*' self-sacrifice for their motherland has often categorically been overlooked to punctuate their rioting, looting, and other (mis)deeds (Bond 2010, 290). 1857 is marked as a symptomatic movement to dismantle the British Empire—it was, in a way, the very reflex of the colonised from the shackles of the coloniser. Counter debate too rages over the nature of such de-colonial movement led by the Indian mutineers. The imperial point of view finds the *sepoy*-revolt ignominious, arguing that there is hardly any glory in firing and plundering 'others' in order to claim independence. It is true that firing or destroying the Redmans' property, for instance, of Shahjahanpur does not glorify their ventures. Whatsoever their conduct is, one cannot, however, ignore the 1857 revolt, what Karl Marx opines, as 'only the reflex, in a concentrated form, of England's own conduct in India [. . .]' (Marx 1857).

In the text, Bond's dismissal of the term 'Eurasian' is anachronistic. But, one may expect that Bond, with his reasonably sound socio-cultural-historical knowledge of his community, quite consciously replaces it. By modernising the old term 'Eurasian' into 'Anglo-Indian', which was commissioned as late as in 1911, he seems to render the great event a human voice, thereby expanding the scope of his novella beyond historiography.

Mariam's Resistance and (Anglo-)Indian Motherhood

The marriage of Mariam's mother, who belonged to an Indian Muslim family, to a French adventurer was habitual sight during British colonial rule, which conducted various schemes to encourage mixed-racial wedlock for imperial convenience. It is also understandable that Mariam's upbringing as Christian in the European culture prioritises patriarchal identity construction over its Indian counterpart. The European descent, despite her quasi-Indian root, makes Mariam a *firangi* woman to the eyes of the agitated *sepoys* of Shahjahanpur. Like a 'pure' European, Mariam is an outsider to the native gaze in spite of her birth and growing-up in India. Her embodied 'western modernity' in spite of her 'domesticated identity' (Blunt 2005, 51) also works to her detriment:

> Anglo-Indian women were seen, and saw themselves, as embodying a distinctively western modernity in debates about the future and status of the community. This modernity spanned their dress, their paid employment beyond the home, and their ability to mix socially with men, to choose whom to marry, and to live in a nuclear rather than a joint family after marriage. Two of these embodied differences have since been reversed in independent India, in that younger Anglo-Indian women now increasingly wear Indian dress and marry men from other Indian communities [. . .]. Such depictions of Anglo-Indian women, and their political mobilization in debates about the uncertain future of the community, served to distance them not only from other Indian women but also from a collective memory of an Indian maternal ancestor. (204–05)

Irony has it that during their stay at Lalaji's house, Mariam and Ruth's Englishness along with that of their other family members has to undergo massive changes. It is also significant to note that an Indian family witnesses the occasion of their alteration of names. Mariam and her family wistfully welcome the change to camouflage their Englishness—which is likely to arouse abhorrence from the mutineers—as an agency of survival. Ruth's voice corroborates:

> Mother also considered it prudent to take Indian names. I was given the name of Khurshid, which is Persian for 'sun', and my cousin Anet, being short of stature, was called Nanni. Pilloo was named Ghulam Hussain, and his mother automatically became known as Ghulam Hussain's mother. Granny was, of course, Baribi. It was easier for us to take Mohammedan names, because we were fluent in Urdu, and because Granny did in fact come from a Muslim family of Rampur. (Bond 2010, 305)

The reception of the Anglo-Indian women has always been enigmatic since the community's emergence; no clear solution is formulated because of active political engagement and interruption. One thing that stands out is that these women are stereotyped negatively. These *memsahibs*, which they were alternatively called, are often depicted as self-centred, snobbish, inactive and frivolous (Caplan 2000, 863). The term *memsahib*, literally meaning 'madam lord', refers to class consciousness and racial hierarchy. 'The memsahib,' Susmita Roye and Rajeshwar Mittapalli point out, 'became both the victim and the beneficiary of the complex situation she found herself in' (2013). They add that even though she 'was acutely aware of her responsibility to advertise her superiority over the native woman', her 'allegiance to her own people [the British]' brought her no remedy (2013). What, therefore, puts the Anglo-Indian female identity into a problematic terrain is the bitter reception by the British/European male-dominated world view.

In *A Flight*, we have observed how the Anglo-Indian women are negatively bracketed in the 'native' households. In the text, there are many who jeer at Mariam and her family. Umda's scathing mockery at Qamran's house, for instance, comes from her ignorance about the British policy during the colonial regime:

> You cannot deny that they [Anglo-Indian women] enjoy laughing and joking with strange men, that they dance and sing, sometimes half-nude, with the arms of strange men round their waists. Then they retire into dark corners where they kiss and are kissed by men other than their husbands! (335)

Umda, Qamran's neighbour, finds it easy to stigmatise them as 'wantons' who 'cannot live without the society of men' (335). Umda's opinion, however, demonstrates in what derogative manner an Anglo-Indian woman's identity can be generalised. Further, her hostility towards all foreign races and her spiteful tendency to consider them in derogatory terms reveals the atrocious face of racial bias. Mariam may represent a Christian family by origin but her awareness of Muslim culture of Shahjahanpur is sound. One, however, could sense that the novelist's concern is not centred on how the Anglo-Indian women become the subject of gossip to the 'natives' but on the system that enables it. The novelist seems to understand that if the 'natives' are accused of being biased, the same can be said of the Anglo-Indians; and in either case, the colonial system by which they have been wronged is curiously overlooked. It is also to be noted that the 1857 Uprising was the first major political move that initiated the process of distancing the mixed-descent people from the 'natives', and it is why they have been a subject of gossip to the 'natives'. If Anglo-Indian women are solely liable for maintaining distance from other Indians, the system of knowledge, by which they are compelled, cannot be discounted. The plight of these Anglo-Indian women thus, at one point, appears to be vulnerable and afflictive in comparison to that of their male counterparts. They consequently have to compromise their Christian identity and play-act like Musalmans so that none can suspect their 'foreign' descent:

> It was in our interests to forget that we had European blood in our veins, and that there was any advantage in the return of the British to power. It was also necessary for us to *seem* to forget that the Christian God was our God, and we allowed it to be believed that we were Muslims. (Bond 2010, 323)

The novelist's focus on Labadoor women, who are in crisis, may thus be read as a conscious act to discern the stereotypic behaviours meted out to Anglo-Indian womanhood in general.

However, while the Muslim women seem submissive in the *zenana,*[4] the *angrejans* appear to be prominent. There is none to argue with Javed;

never does his wife dare question his decision. This is why Mariam's constant rejoinders both hurt his male ego and assuage his arrogance. Earlier, when Javed Khan with his band of henchmen, intruded Lala's house in search of the *firangans*, Mariam's rebellious stance checked the Pathan's wrath: 'If you would take my daughter's life, take mine before hers, I beg of you by the sword of Ali' (Bond 2010, 313). Javed would disclose later how Mariam's courage enticed him, arousing a certain respect for her. In Javed's house, Mariam's reply to Khan Begam regarding Ruth's birth as 'the offspring of an Englishman' and her immediate anecdote 'only Allah knows what will become of us all, for there is no one left to protect us' (315) pacifies Kothiwali but in no way discourages Javed's temptation to marry Ruth. Amidst racial hostility and class discrepancy, Javed's house is a fine instance of inter-caste and inter-religious coalescence. Javed's stepmother is a low-caste woman who, with her 'large and pretty eyes' charmed her father. His uncle married Kothiwali, who came from a low-caste Hindu family. Javed's family is hospitable to its guests too. The Anglo-Indian women are immediately welcomed, sympathised with and taken care of. Mariam's unwillingness to attend the Muslim prayer is never questioned; rather, this can be viewed as a meaningful marker to pursue religious tolerance. The Indian households, similar to Dehra's bazaar, can accommodate cross-cultural practices. Carrying on with our discussion, in order to dissuade intoxicated Javed, Mariam invests all her verbal tactics, for instance, how can a Muslim marry a Christian? Again, in Qamran's house, these *firangans* confront Badran, another superstitious young woman with an acid tongue. Ruth describes her as 'a spiteful young woman, with a sharp, lashing tongue, very hostile towards all foreign races. She had been very displeased at our introduction into the family, always gave us angry looks, and never missed an opportunity to speak ill of us' (334). According to Ruth, Badran's attitude instigates Umda to scandalise the entire *firangi* race.

Javed Khan's intention to marry Ruth is evident. When Kothiwali, Javed's aunt, tries to argue with her nephew by arguing that they are of good birth, and that Khan Begam is an agreeable wife, Javed cannot but express his fascination with Ruth:

> The very first time I saw her [in her father's house], I was struck by her beauty. She shone like Zohra, the morning star. Looking at her now, I realize the truth of the saying that a flower never looks so beautiful as when it is on its parent stem. (Bond 2010, 316)

Although his command in stirred-up situations may devalorise his credibility and picturise him as a ruffian, Javed's concern in protecting the 'white women' in distress discloses his human side as well, at least to Ruth. Her secret desire for Javed's manly presence is revealed in the final lines of the novel:

> Looking back on those months when we were his prisoners, I cannot help feeling a sneaking admiration for him. He was very wild and muddle-headed, and often cruel, but he was also very handsome and gallant, and there was in him a streak of nobility which he did his best to conceal. (368)

Mariam's strategic ploy, however, accentuates Kothiwali's effort to avert her married nephew's sudden desire:

> What I wanted to bring home to you is that if you are such an admirer of beauty, your Khan-Begum is neither ugly nor dark. I should have thought *Firangi* women had blue eyes and fair hair, but these poor things—how frightened they look!—would pass off as one of us! (317)

The reference to the 'blue eyes' takes us back to the context where women with blue eyes were once regarded something ominous and women with fair hair were related to witches. Both 'blue eyes' and 'fair hair' collectively put a *firangi* woman in the position of an enchantress or a siren. But having seen them closely, Kothiwali, the spokesperson of the 'native' women, understands that these Anglo-Indian women are not much different from them. Further evidence to the changing of 'native' perspective is noticed in Javed's elder sister, Qamran's house, where they are invited as guests. The narratorial voice informs us how Qamran, renouncing her prejudiced view, accepts them as family members:

> Whereas they had formerly believed that, as *Firangi* women, we would be peeping out of doors and windows in order to be seen by men, without whose society European women were supposed to be unable to live, they were agreeably surprised to find that we delighted in hard work, that we loved needles and thread, and that, far from seeking the company of men, we did our best to avoid them. (334)

The narrative also comments on internal disturbance—be it personal, political, or household issues. If, on the one side, it renders a comprehensive picture of the superstitions, difficulties, biases, sentiments and aspirations of Muslim women behind the *zenana*, on the other side, it suggests how British class consciousness allows them to stereotypically imagine Anglo-Indian women. Javed's wife, like an Anglo-Indian woman, is marginalised. But, any assessment of Khan-*Begum* and Mariam on the same ground will narrow down the latter's degree of crisis. Khan-*Begum* does not have the verbal ploy that Mariam has; but she does not also need to negotiate the anxiety of Anglo-Indianness and situational agony for survival that the latter is destined with. Mariam's flair, composed tone, and strategic diplomacy in arguing with the other Indians are meant not merely to save their lives but also to resist generalisation. Their adaptability has been tested quite a number of times in the course of action. Their abduction by determined Javed at Lalaji's absence may hint at the supremacy of patriarchy, but Javed's befuddlement at Mariam's sudden fury and true feeling for Ruth change the direction of such apprehension. Javed now assures Mariam: 'I shall strike off the heads of half a dozen before a hair on my *Firangan*'s head can be touched' (Bond 2010, 328). Mariam's success lies not in safeguarding her daughter and earning respect from magnanimous Javed but in subverting stereotypical paradigms. We have thus observed how Javed's behaviour from the role of a kidnapper to a protector has changed dramatically vis-à-vis Mariam's valour. Nupur Chaudhuri substantiates that the Anglo-Indian women, far from being passive and lazy, 'behaved courageously when faced with crises such as the Sepoy Mutiny or Afgan Wars' (Chaudhuri 1988, 518).

Locating the 'White Woman' Identity: *Memsahib* under Mimicry?

The narrative, as I have already pointed out, invokes a complex history with which the reception of Anglo-Indian woman identity is intertwined. Indrani Sen while reviewing MacMillan's book *Women of the Raj* (1988) comments that:

> No study on the English woman in India seems to be quite complete without a discussion of the 1857 revolt. This is primarily because for 19th century colonial discourse '1857' has become a site for colonial myth-making. Hysterical myths about the white woman's sexual vulnerability and fragility as well as her abuse at the hands of the 'lustful' Indian were constructed around that event. (Sen 1990, 102)

Such British self-fashioning of the 1857 historical context in India was not very uncommon before independence. Sharing mixed-descent lineage and being a well-read scholar, Ruskin Bond understands the misconception revolving around their reception and, intelligibly, his novel undertakes a voice in favour of an Anglo-Indian woman. It is, therefore, likely that Bond, who has always revolted against racial identification, seeks for an uninhibited perspective. By foregrounding the active engagement of an Anglo-Indian woman, *A Flight* upholds, circuitously but steadfastly, the experience and consequent dilemma of Anglo-Indian women in colonial India. The text also challenges the stigma, such as that of a 'fallen woman' associated with mixed-race women. By calling the expression 'fallen woman' to be the 'most potent and lasting trope of femininity surrounding the [Sepoy] Rebellion' and production 'in the male narratives of 1857', Grace Amelia Watts shows how they are also manoeuvred to be the 'product of a heavily gendered discourse in which women were conspicuously silenced' (Watts 2014, 179). As a representative of Indo-European hybrid culture, Anglo-Indian women were already considered mentally deficient by the time of the mid-19th century. Such direct accusation regarding their moral weakness was considered as 'inherent in their blood' (Caplan, 'Iconographies' 867). It is the fact that their morality, demeanours and conducts were judged singularly on the ground of their *métis* origin. However, the coloniser did not alone stigmatise these women. The gaze of the colonised too was derogatory. To understand this stigmatisation, let us briefly understand the sociopolitical backdrop.

It is not unknown to the novelist that Anglo-Indian women were treated with a degree of suspicion. The notion that the Anglo-Indian woman is without 'moral fibre' has been a common trope. Of late, a major reason why Anjan Dutt's 2004 film *Bow Barracks Forever* generates apathy from the Anglo-Indian community in Kolkata is that the film, despite the director's earnestness, reproduces 'earlier British stereotypes of their sexual proclivities' (Caplan 2000, 878) and sidelines their individual will to associate with Kolkata. In addition to such a tendency, Anglo-Indian history and sustenance were manoeuvred in the 19th century narrative: 'Not only in intermarriage or, for that matter, concubinage disapproved of, but, as Greenberger has noted, whenever a story features a liaison between a European man and Indian woman, the (Anglo-Indian) children born of a such a union are not allowed to survive' (867). Although this minority community resulted from British proclivities, the British were later worried by the increase of these 'half-caste' people. The British ensured some policies to restrict or limit this racially mixed, 'low-caste' other in order to maintain their privileged, 'pure' position. But with the upsurge of internal conflicts and hierarchical challenges within the subcontinent, the British failed to pay much heed but categorically distanced themselves from them. Added to the British hostility towards the mixed-blood, imperial narratives served as a fence to safeguard the former by putting further affliction on the latter for survival. Imperial writing, moreover, continued to locate the Anglo-Indian women 'as an impediment to the male enterprise of empire-building' (Sen 1990, 101).

In some native households of Shahjahanpur, Anglo-Indians are viewed as careless, unworthy and licentious and their entry causes a stir in the *mohalla* in the same way that Mariam's entry into Javed's house to find a suitable match for her daughter causes a stir. Their preferences worked together to incite such tropes. The Anglo-Indians would prefer to talk in English and carry forward an English lifestyle. However distinctive their tonal quality is from the British, they are basically *angrez* to the 'native' gaze, especially during the colonial regime. Simultaneously, their tendency to follow the latest European fashion, like the British, generates sneers from the ruling class. While talking about the reception of Anglo-Indian women Erica Lewin initiates her article 'Anglo-Indian Women: Identity Issues' (1996) by asking how an Anglo-Indian woman can be located, or on what ground their identity dilemma can be justified. Their constant negotiation, she argues, between the coloniser and the colonised creates 'an "in-between" space in postcolonial debate':

> Anglo-Indian women claim both an 'Anglo' and an 'Indian' heritage [. . .] they do not perceive themselves as either 'Anglo' or 'Indian' solely [. . .]. They constantly refer to this basic notion of racial hybridity in their discussion about their identities. This biological factor challenges the binary of the west vs. east and self vs. other. Anglo-Indian women self-identify with both sides of these binaries with a simultaneous affirmation of their Anglo-Indian heritage. (5)

Mariam and her family's constant shift of abodes under compulsion—from the house of Ramjimal to that of Javed Khan to a barely habitable house in the village of Indarkha under the hospitality of a Bengali-Muslim doctor—affect them both at psychological and physical levels. Their adaptability, indeed, in sociopolitical tensions upholds a great sense of mental strength. Their endurance, nonetheless, raises a pertinent issue. It is true that adaptability is necessary and instrumental for selfhood; the more they adapt, the more they reflect the sense of resistance. But the irony lies in the fact that this resistance determines their eligibility of belongingness in their own motherland, delimiting their identity as colonised subject.

We may consider Mariam's doubly-enunciated position by drawing on Homi Bhabha's notion of 'double vision' in his essay 'Of Mimicry and Man' (1994, 122). Mimicry, Bhabha theorises, is that ambivalent position and trained imitation by which the colonised expresses his subservience to and follows the white/coloniser. Since Mariam, at least racially, is not a 'pure' Indian native, her Anglo-Indian womanhood is doubly marginalised, just as the Third-World subaltern woman is doubly colonised through the brutality of colonialism and patriarchy. In other words, the Anglo-Indian woman's identity is trapped in the politics of colonisation and patriarchal tropes. The racial hierarchy by the British construes her as unequal in the first place, while male-oriented (or, the British-fabricated) myths and stereotypical attributes also subordinate her. The initial hatred of the 'natives' towards Mariam and her family comes from these sources. What accentuates this is the class arrogance of some of the Anglo-Indian women. Indrani Sen explains the point in her study:

> Undoubtedly, in a colonial context, race would be a central factor in the exercise of power. MacMillan notes that even the poor, oppressed barrack wives displayed feelings of racial superiority solely by virtue of belonging to the ruling race. Yet it is demonstrably not the *sole* factor, for the 'memsahib' has been customarily taken to task by historians not only for her racism but also for her class arrogance. (Sen 1990, 102)

As a voice of the Anglo-Indian female identity, Mariam's subordination, first by the sociopolitical and cultural hyphenation and second by stereotypical/patriarchal representation, can be further understood from Nupur Chaudhuri's observation:

> The memsahib in India, like her counterpart in Britain, commonly derived her status from her husband's occupation; her social position was clearly defined by her husband's rank in the colonial administrative system. The social hierarchy was strictly maintained by the unwritten rule limiting a British wife to her husband's sphere of social acquaintances. (1988, 519)

Such positioning on her part is ambiguous because more than often the Anglo-Indian woman is wrongly imagined by the colonial discourse to reinforce the very idea of hyphenation, which in turn asserts racial supremacy and class superiority. Read closely, Mariam's image as 'wanton', as described by Umda, is not the latter's own voice, rather the very outcome of the way an Anglo-Indian woman is strategically portrayed. By supporting the ruling class morally during the Sepoy Uprising of 1857, the Anglo-Indians started losing trust from their 'native' friends. Umda's notion is partially biased because her perception is clouded by the prevailing discourse; her impression is partially true because the enclosure makes the Anglo-Indian woman's identity an object of enigma to the other Indians.

On the basis of the Anglo-Indian woman's doubly-silenced state, effected both by the British class superiority and patriarchy, a comparative study with the subaltern woman may be generated. The former's 'mimic' stance or adopted attitude situates her in a superior position to the 'native' gaze, which, in turn, complicates her marginal emplacement as a subaltern. Whereas the subaltern woman is doubly silenced both by the ruling class and colonised male, this is not simply the case with the Anglo-Indian woman due to her double-inheritance. If the Third-World woman is particularly colonised by the patriarchy, the dilemma of the Anglo-Indian woman is even more baffling.

Although Mariam is well received by Kothiwali, what impedes Umda from receiving Mariam whole-heartedly as one of their own is her ignorance of colonial history. From her lifestyle to food habit, religion to dress-code, Mariam is associated with European conduct. But the 1857 Uprising puts her at the mercy of the 'natives', forcing this hapless Anglo-Indian stand vis-à-vis a dubious juncture from where she hardly escapes. Mimicry, as Bhabha maintains, appears as 'one of the most elusive and effective strategies of colonial power and knowledge' (1994, 122) to camouflage the coloniser's deceptive act of removing the ladder from the ground. It is the very ladder that once brought the Anglo-Indian closer to the ruling class. Once the interest is over, the connecting ladder is withdrawn; and the traumatic denouement is the 'mimic' stature of the Anglo-Indian who is now left open to be questioned: 'The effect of mimicry on the authority of colonial discourse is profound and disturbing. For in "normalizing" the colonial state or subject, the dream of post-Enlightenment civility alienates its own language of liberty and produces another knowledge of its norms' (123). It results in, Bhabha adds, 'the colonial subject as a "partial" presence. By "partial" I mean both "incomplete" and "virtual"' (123). Thus, 'mimicry is at once resemblance and menace' (123). The other local Indians of Shahjahanpur, in general, feel similar 'resemblance' and 'menace' from the *firangans*. The social segregation of the Anglo-Indians induces suspicion from the 'natives', whereas the ruling Englishmen keep themselves detached from the Anglo-Indians. The novelist's approach, however, alters Mariam's historically-originated 'mimic' emplacement and locates her as an individual Indian woman whose courage is to be registered. Mariam is, after all, a victim, who is caught between quasi-Indian and quasi-European self. Thus, towards the end of the novel, if her departure from Shahjahanpur to her brother's secure abode implies 'ambivalence', it also vivifies the image of a flight of pigeons, symbolising that restoration of peace is yet to come.

The Humanitarian Drive: Intersecting Border-Relation

A Flight of Pigeons turns out to be more profound due to the juxtaposition of cruelty and compassion—if violence anguishes innocent Anglo-Indians, kindness replaces their wound. It is not unknown to us about the merciless fatal injury done to Mr Labadoor. We have also seen how Ramjimal's earnest assay helps Mariam and her family to survive. He may be a 'lean' man with 'a long moustache', but his surefooted presence and dignified speech bring forth 'an air of determination' (Bond 2010, 300) of the rarest kind, which earns admiration from the women in distress. This Hindu businessman is one who, on being questioned about his decision to protect the *angrejans* in his house, clarifies his moral responsibility unhesitatingly: '"I have done what is right [. . .]. I have not given shelter to *Angrezans*. I have given shelter to friends. Let people say or think as they please"' (300). If Ramjimal's support for Mariam and her family comes from neighbourly concern, it, on a broader aspect, anticipates the way of paying dues for the cruelty done by fellow Indians. Later in the text, we hear him speak to Javed Khan: 'It was very wrong of you to enter my house during my absence and bring away my guests without my permission. Had I been there, you could only have done so by making your way over my dead body' (320). The guardian of Mariam and her family is now replaced, and with this, they are to negotiate with Javed's desire. With this alteration, however, the tale takes a different turn as Mariam, being the representative of her family, is to prove her mental strength against all odds. The 'native' households, however, are not altogether against them. As we have noticed how Hafiz's presence resists her neighbouring aunt Umda, who speaks ill against the *firangans*.

Javed Khan is an Indian 'native', but his inflicting attitudes emplace him initially as a don to these helpless women until Ruth recognizes his romantic traits. In the prologue to the novel, the novelist describes Javed as 'a person of some importance in the bazaars of Shahjahanpur', who undertakes 'any exploit of a dangerous nature, provided the rewards were [are] high' (Bond 2010, 290). He is well aware of English law and can easily eclipse the British authority because none dares identify him. A courageous man, Javed is a strong competitor for the British. But his act of snatching the *angrejans* away from Ramjimal's house out of wrath and then to fulfil his intention to marry Ruth Labadoor immediately serves as a testimony to his gesture in telescopic view and delimits him as a ruffian. It is also to be mentioned that Javed's antagonistic stance, however debatable it may sound, makes Mariam's struggle more articulate. Javed may give Mariam space to consider her daughter's marriage with him, but his proposal, if we call it so, is conditioned by situational advantage and verbal audacity. The change of power-politics between the British emperor and the abrupt control by the *sepoys* amidst political agitation of the late 1850s, in a way, commodify the Anglo-Indian women in particular. Ruth's case in Shahjahanpur exemplifies how an Anglo-Indian subject becomes an object of desire to someone in power. Simultaneously, a counter study makes its entry clear from the very first chapter of the novel with Ruth's observation immediately after she witnesses her father's demise:

> Leaving him against the stone wall of the church, I ran round to the vestry side and almost fell over Mr. Ricketts, who was lying about twelve feet from the vestry door [. . . .]. Sick with horror, I turned from the spot and began running home through Buller's compound.
>
> Nobody met me on the way. No one challenged me or tried to intercept or molest me. The cantonment seemed empty and deserted; but just as I reached the end of Buller's compound, I saw our house in flames. I stopped at the gate, looking about for my mother, but could not see her anywhere. Granny, too, was missing, and the servants. Then I saw Lala Ramjimal walking down the road towards me. (Bond 2010, 295)

Ruth's ordeal begins after her father's untimely death at the hands of ignited mutineers when all of her family members are left at the mercy of local Indians for their lives. Although the novella's preface unveils that the tale is narrated by Ruth, it is, in fact, the novelist's memorisation of his father's oral narration of a true incident, which Aubrey Bond had heard from his father. This change of narrators is important for two reasons: first, by letting Ruth narrate the tale the novelist could easily transfix his identity in her because both their fathers had to sacrifice their lives during the service for the Raj: 'Bond's imagined identification with Ruth's position is supplemented by a sense of alienation he suffered on a couple of occasions during his childhood when he had to confront native ire in forms of scornful invectives and physical assault' (Bandyopadhyay 2012, 94). Second,

Bond's looking back to the 1850s–60s context and his sincerity in history come not as an 'antiquarian' (White 1978, 41) but to locate himself as the product of the British Empire. By retelling Ruth's personal ordeals and outcomes, the authorial self, perhaps unknown to himself, recasts his own past and reassesses his own dilemmas.

Although the 1857 *sepoy* rebellion, kindled by the then socio-political environments, caused agitations among the 'natives' against the Europeans, the exceptional humane attitude by some of the 'natives' such as Ramjimal towards the hapless *angrez* must be taken into consideration because history has several instances like this. In his study, Debashis Bandyopadhyay perceptively notes:

> Bond highlights these acts of tolerance and, far from committing any travesty of truth; he underlines the essence of humanity that would account for restoring sangfroid to his own disturbed sense of identity. The retelling of the tale, for him, is a therapeutic act. He certainly finds assuagement for his concerns ofbelonging—repressed in the unsavoury memory of racial snipe and battering—by vicariously enacting the drama of self-definition in Mariam and her daughter. (2012, 96)

Humanity, truly speaking, always gives Bond's writing certain directness. Humanity, for him, is sustenance—an outlook, a living entity. It is one such shaping spirit that has evolved in his works over the years. Bond clarifies his motive in the text's Introduction:

> In retelling the tale for today's reader I attempted to bring out the common humanity of most of the people involved—for in times of conflict and inter-religious or racial hatred, there are always a few (just a few) who are prepared to come to the aid of those unable to defend themselves. (Bond 2010, 289)

It must be mentioned that Mrs Labadoor's present plight is not because of her mixed-descent but by British ploy and the misjudgement of the agitated *sepoys*. Bond's narrative, in fact, presents a terrain in which the demarcation between a Third-World woman and an Anglo-Indian woman is compared and contested. Like the doubly-silenced stance of the Third-World woman, the Anglo-Indian woman too occupies a marginalised position. As a *firangan*, moreover, Mariam is destined to fall into double barricades. Mariam's reception both at the British and Indian eyes is complicated, where she has to prove her European identity and Indian consciousness:

> Her predicament—which is something of a double-edged sword—resembles that of angst-ridden James Skinner, one of the landed gentlemen of 1850s Delhi who suffered for his mixed blood, traceable to a Scottish father and a Rajput mother. Skinner fought bravely in the Maratha army only to be ejected from their ranks because his father was British; later in the British army, he was increasingly discriminated against for his Indian blood. It is worth noting that the possibility of Ruth and her mother being rescued by the British is left suspended. They end their flight at Bharatpur in the shelter of Mariam's Anglo-Indian brother; and in their final escape they are aided by Nasim Khan and a Sikh soldier. (Bandyapadhyay 2012, 99)

Despite all these supportive conditions, one cannot ignore Mariam's valiance. Mariam's social alacrity, moral values, dignified Urdu pronunciation and *kalma*, considerable knowledge of Indian folklore, iconic manoeuvre in racially and politically charged situations and presence of mind in situational crisis present her as a sure-footed, self-disciplined and upright woman. Her indomitable stance to protect her daughter from Javed Khan's unyielding desire may be seen, to borrow from Parama Roy, a portrayal of Mother India, who is committed 'to everyday heroism' (1998, 150).

The way Mariam handles racial prejudice, a cardinal issue among the Anglo-Indians in Shahjahanpur, demands our attention. When Mariam Labadoor comes out of her egocentricity and befriends Lala Ramjimal and other 'natives', the class-consciousness breaks down. It is her characteristic significance to elude racial boundaries even before the 1857 agitation at Shahjahanpur begins. She feels no qualms in gossiping with her servants or vendors—the so-called 'lower class', according to the coloniser. Unlike the racially biased British/Anglo-Indian, Mariam gathers an insider's sense of value, which, to a certain degree, comes from her (quasi-)Indian inheritance and upbringing in India. Her decision to avoid Dr Bowling's party on the eve of the massacre or her prudence to discourage her husband and daughter to attend the usual Sunday morning prayers at St. Mary's may surprise readers at first glance, but such awareness is possible from socialisation. The narrative point of view ensures Mariam's effortless identification with Indian sensibilities. Her immediate thought of suicide in the well after losing her husband establishes the sentiment of a Hindu wife. Her constant protection of Ruth from imminent ordeals highlights her motherly concern. In Bond's vision, Mariam, a mixed-descent by origin, is unavoidably Indian. It seems that the novelist does not really wish to see her as anything but an Indian—through which we can gauge her maternal image. In her final journey to Bharatpur, Mariam, on being confronted by some anonymous mutineers, gallantly raises her knife as self-defence and unnerves them by questioning: 'Is there anything unusual about seeing so many helpless females fleeing from the city to escape dishonour and death?' (Bond 2010, 366). Mariam's stance is so iconic that Gangaram, the bullock-cart driver, cannot but express his admiration: 'You are weak in body, but have the spirit of a goddess!' (367).

The text may be read as a commentary on femininity and masculinity, or femininity over patriarchy. Mariam's resistance against the local hooligan Javed Khan and the latter's subjugation, Ruth's usage of 'Mother' with a capital 'M' in her father's absence, the successive ordeals and adjustment in a male-dominated society and Indian *zenana* claim the victory of Mariam's femininity and motherhood. Mariam judiciously guesses that manly Javed is inclined to obey the code of asking permission to a male parent of the bride—the code formulated by patriarchal law. Mariam's bravery lies not merely in such protest or in questioning Javed Khan's stance but also in endurance. Her patience for a favourable situation makes the character so integral and crucial. The novel thus lionises her motherhood. As a mother figure, Mariam's deterring act to outwit Javed's voyeurism is meant not merely to protect Ruth from his desire but as a dissent.

A Flight of Pigeons, therefore, stands for the liberty of an Anglo-Indian/Eurasian woman in the Indian context. And, the novelist's intention to identify Mariam with the intrinsic Indian (be it a Hindu or Muslim) values underscores the very idea of Indian liberalness and ensures cultural variances. In Bond's text, the Anglo-Indian women are no longer the objects of lascivious male onlookers but common Indians. *A Flight* also dethrones those prejudiced narratives that flaunt and prioritise 'pure'/European white women over their mixed-blood counterpart. By raising the politics of mixed-racial marginality, this novel necessitates an 'intrusion' with a humane message. Although it is hard to imagine whether there is a *pir* (a wandering hermit) in the story's factual account, in Bond's text the *pir* appears as a humanitarian voice and advises Javed khan to be nice to the Anglo-Indian women. The ending, as discussed earlier, shows Mariam's return to safe placidity out of the terrain of agitation. If Mariam's move for a 'quiet and orderly life' to her brother's household at Bharatpur (368) questions the textual motive, one may also consider that she is given freedom to follow her will. Since Bond's narrative almost always focuses on the individual, Ruth's story may not be the sole reflection of the Anglo-Indian community of the day, but after all a story with historical authenticity. That is, Mariam's desire to go beyond the racial and class biases and blend with everyday Indianness may not be the only picture of the Anglo-Indian community, but this is not impossible. It appears that Ruskin Bond sees the Uprising, not in exclusive terms of different 'isms' but as a human event of extraordinary outcomes, which, what William Dalrymple observes, enables one to revive an ordinary fate caught up in one of the great upheavals of history: 'It is through the human stories of the successes, struggles, grief, anguish and despair of these individuals that we can best bridge the great chasm of time and understanding separating us from the remarkably different world of mid-nineteenth-century India' (2006, 13).

A Flight of Pigeons voices an anti-stereotypical viewpoint by exploring interracial interaction and shows how a mixed-blood woman, even in the mid-19th century, associates with the Indian 'natives'. Mariam may have been brought up as Christian but her understanding of Indian sensibilities arising out of her direct knowledge of Muslim values and contact with the other Indians makes her an insider. Mariam's social life is, in fact, the furtherance of Rusty's mixing with the bazaar boys in *The Room* in order to appreciate the spirit of intellectual pluralism that Bond's texts generate.

Notes

1. Native is placed within quotes here, and throughout the chapter, because the context is different. The narrative is based in 19th-century colonial India. Mark that I have also used 'other' before the expression.
2. Bond used to visit the Old Committee Room of Mussoorie Library to take notes. The information is based on the author's personal interview with the novelist on 6 April 2016.
3. It is unclear whether Ruskin Bond means Bahadur Shah Zafar, the then Mughal emperor, who having realised that his dynasty was on the verge of extinction blessed the *sepoys*. For more, see William Dalrymple's *The Last Mughal* (2006).
4. *Zenana* refers to a particular section of a house reserved for the women of the family.

Bibliography

Bandyopadhyay, Debashis. 2012. *Locating the Anglo-Indian Self in Ruskin Bond: A Postcolonial Review*. New Delhi: Anthem.

Bond, Ruskin. 1992. *Strange Men Strange Places*. New Delhi: Rupa.

———. 2010. 'A Flight of Pigeons'. *Classic Ruskin Bond Vol 1: The Novels*. New Delhi: Penguin, 287–370.

Bhabha, Homi K. 1994. *The Location of Culture*. New York: Routledge.

Blunt, Alison. 2005. *Domicile and Diaspora: Anglo-Indian Women and the Spatial Politics of Home*. Oxford, MA: Blackwell.

Caplan, Lionel. 2000. 'Iconographies of Anglo-Indian Women: Gender Constructs and Contrasts in a Changing Society', *Modern Asian Studies*, 34(4): 863–92. Available at: JSTOR (accessed on 13 May 2016).

Chaudhuri, Nupur. 1988. 'Memsahibs and Motherhood in Nineteenth-Century Colonial India', *Victorian Studies*, 31(4): 517–35. Available at: JSTOR (accessed on 13 May 2017).

Dalrymple, William. 2006. *The Last Mughal: The Fall of a Dynasty, Delhi, 1857*. Gurgaon: Penguin.

Kohli, Devindra. 2005. 'Ruskin Bond'. In *Encyclopedia of Post-Colonial Literatures in English*, edited by Eugene Benson and L.W. Conolly, 131–32. London: Routledge, Available at: Google Book Search (accessed on 13 May 2016).

Lewin, Erica. 1996. 'Anglo Indian women: Identity issues'. *The International Journal of Anglo Indian Studies*, 1(2): 3–12.

Marx, Karl. 1857. 'The Indian Revolt'. *Marxists Internet Archive. New-York Daily Tribune*, 16 September, n.pag. Available at: https://www.marxists.org/archive/marx/works/1857/09/16.htm (accessed on 17 May 2016).

Mukherjee, Meenakshi. 1985. *Realism and Reality: The Novel and Society in India*. New Delhi: Oxford University Press.

Nayar, Pramod K., ed. 2007. *The Penguin 1857 Reader*. Gurgaon: Penguin.

Roy, Parama. 1998. *Indian Traffic: Identities in Question in Colonial and Postcolonial India*. USA: University of California Press.

Roye, Susmita and Rajeshwar Mittapalli, eds. 2013. 'Introduction: (Re)Viewing the Gaze'. *The Male Empire Under the Female Gaze: The British Raj and the Memsahib*. Amherst, NY: Cambria Press, n.pag. Available at: Google Book Search (accessed on 5 December 2015).

Sen. Indrani, rev. 1990.'"Memsahibs": Woman in "Purdah"'. *Women of the Raj: The Mothers, Wives, and Daughters of the British Empire in India* by Margaret MacMillan. *Economic and Political Weekly*, January: 101–02.

Watts, Grace Amelia. 2014. 'Can the Memsahib Speak? A Re-Examination of the Tropes and Stereotypes Surrounding the Anglo-Indian Female During the Indian Rebellion of 1857'. *The South Asianist*, 3(1): 178–208. Available at: http://www.southasianist.ed.ac.uk/article/viewFile/238/1606 (accessed on 9 May 2016).

White, Hayden. 1978. *Tropics of Discourse*. Baltimore, MD: John Hopkins University Press.

5

Dehra

Return to Roots in *A Handful of Nuts*

In the previous chapter, I have discussed how the local households of Shahjahanpur, like Dehra's bazaar in *The Room on the Roof*, induce cultural intersection. Just as Rusty's journey to the bazaar foregrounds negotiation of the self, Shahjahanpur's domestic space allows self-transformative ground to Mariam. *A Handful of Nuts* (2010), with its setting also generates an *adda* space by allowing the narrator's evolving identity to progress towards firmer occupancy in India. In *Small Towns, Big Stories* (2017), Bond seems to justify his reliance on small locality as setting:

> Oddly enough, although I spent three years in London and five in New Delhi, those great cities never gave me much by way of stories. It is easier to know people in small places. Sometimes you can't help knowing them. [. . .] There's yet another advantage to writing about small places. You might get writer's block living in Delhi or Mumbai, but in small town India you won't run out of tales to tell. Like it or not, you are a part of human comedy. (x)

A Handful of Nuts is a tale of intimacy with the day to day specificities of Dehra's (Dehradun's) mid-1950s, where the novelist is intoxicated with, what Alice Truax finds in Amit Chaudhuri, 'the enduring allure of the everyday' (2015). This fond sense of daily existence, indeed, puts his narrative near to life. Here the characters are entwined with ordinary comforts and treated in such leisurely manner that they set themselves free from narrative jostles and live with an innate and intuitive understanding of the world called Dehra. Bond's Dehra is almost perfectly still, yet its presence is always felt. The novelist shows no urgency to introduce the town; it is rather familiarised through its characters. This is precisely why Dehra, in Bondian oeuvre, is so provoking even when nothing really happens here. While commenting on choosing a locale for his book, author-critic Saikat Majumdar reveals why his setting, despite his long stay in America, fails to find an equivalent space there:

> Because, I now realize, that is the period when one forms a relation with place that is non-intellectual, raw, and visceral, or at least predominantly so, full of primal joys and terrors, sensual memories, absurd connections made on the basis of daily habits and bodily experience. (2017)

This helps us conceive why Ruskin Bond's debut novel, despite its fictional genesis in Britain, needed a firm ground for creative adequacy. In *A Handful of Nuts*, in relying on Dehra's cultural space, Bond allows no moral suspicion. Otherwise, the possible danger is that Dehra could have easily been unnoticed in the intrusion of a big city or in an unintelligible environment; that is to say, the small-town cosmopolitanism of Dehra might not be appropriated to Dehradun's city-space. The latent contestation of Dehra's old sense of being with that of the present is evident, even though they technically coincide. The novelist's preoccupation with the 1950s' Dehra emerges both from an instinctive engagement with its physical setting and the yearning to emplace his 21-year-old self into fictional realities, drawn from lived experiences so that a true reflection of identity can be conceived. Unlike the other works discussed in this book, *A Handful of Nuts* obliquely meditates on how Dehra's culture-space appreciates the narrator's sense of belonging in India. The concern of the present chapter is thus intertwined with the textual representation of Dehra's everyday cultural variances.

In Bond's authorial inquiry, 'Dehra' is preferred to 'Dehradun' because the former presents a fine convergence of the past and the present, the public and the private, the objective and the subjective, as corroborating its relevance to the semi-autobiographical identity of the author. To drive the point home, we are engaged with the novelist's mature handling of the timeframe that casually draws us back to the milieu, as if nothing has changed. Apprehension can be raised if such an endeavour fails considerably, or the ease of narrative acumen while delineating Dehra's daily scenes goes otherwise. But the narrative thrust unfailingly condenses Bond's expressions of Indianness. We are therefore directed to a rich journey to Dehra's quotidian world which, far from being misleading, depicts small-town sentiments, superstitions, biases, failures and aspirations.

In a recent issue called 'Little India', published by the *American Book Review* in 2015, Saikat Majumdar persuasively points out in his introductory article how the coalescing between the provincial and the cosmopolitan denotes much beyond 'hostile binaries': 'As the finest achievements of literary modernism reveal, the most exciting life of cosmopolitanism is paradoxically embodied in its provincial incarnation' (4). In the same issue, Tabis Khair's essay, specifying the dynamics between small-town and city, carries forward a compelling argument, from where the present discussion can fairly be initiated. Taking a cue from Arvind Adiga's *The White Tiger* (2008), Khair reads the 1970s–80s Gaya, a small Indian town in the state of Uttar Pradesh and a place where he grew up, as a half-baked town with 'half-baked opinions and aspirations' (5). He elucidates that '[i]f cosmopolitanism is a lived ability to engage with and accept difference, then I would argue that half-baked small towns contain types of cosmopolitanism that are rendered invisible from metropolitan perspectives. I feel I grew up as a cosmopolitan person as much *because* of half-baked Gaya as *despite* it' (5). The seeming contradiction between provincialism and cosmopolitanism in a small-town is clarified by his concluding remark: 'Just as metropolises—given the vast scope of seclusion that they offer—may encourage provincialism, small towns can also give rise to cosmopolitanism' (5). Following what Khair argues, Dehra in *A Handful of Nuts* can be seen as a half-baked town with dashed hopes and half-fulfilled desires, which might not be equally resonant with the rapid urbanisation of Dehradun.

When Ruskin Bond returned to Dehra's cultural milieu in 1955[1] after having been temporarily marooned in an alien land, a sense of tranquillity pervaded his being, *A Handful of Nuts* being its collaborative evidence. Curiously, nowhere in this novel does the author-speaker call 'Dehra' 'Dehradun' in spite of its fictionalisation in the mid-1990s, lest the years-old affinity be affected. 'Dehra' is sufficient to (re)locate him in renewing self-confidence in the Indian context:

> Back to sleepy Dehra, somnolent in the hot afternoon sun and humid from the recent rain. Dragonflies hovered over the canals. Mosquitoes bred in still waters, multiplying their own species and putting a brake on ours. Someone at the bus stand told me that the Maharani was down with malaria; as a result I walked through the bazaar with a spring in my step, even though my cheap new chappals were cutting into the flesh between my toes. Underfoot, the neem-pods gave out their refreshing though pungent odour. This was home, even though it did not offer fame or riches. (Bond 2010, 486)

Dehra, in this text, thus evokes quotidian life, which subtly fills the nooks of Bond's youthful consciousness. The town's space, no less intimate than his private 'room', becomes a site of self-knowledge (just like the *chaat*-shop *adda* in *The Room on the Roof*) and existence—a site of re-establishing present connection with the days gone by. In his unceasing literary oeuvre, this north-Indian town is caught both in the timely and the untimely, the linear and the cyclical, the temporal and the timeless. Although the urge to bring back the space of his younger days is ever present, the author is aware that old days cannot be eternal. Dehradun's dynamic (s)pace to Bond in the post-War period, especially from the 1960s onwards, fails to generate the 'mood' conducive to create an agreeable setting for this narrative. Dehradun also fails to induce the moral universe that Dehra is capable of. Therefore, travelling down memory lane, the novelist tries to retrieve the personal memories of 'bicycles and pony-drawn tongas' (2008, vii). In the 1960s, the author's practical yet reluctant move from Dehra to Delhi and consequently to Mussoorie was hastened by a latent complaint against his favourite town. Bond is not against progress; yet he cannot help bemoaning over the loss of Dehra's aesthetic coherence, climate and other cultural delicacies. The author-narrator also misses the fond company of the town-turned-city.

The authorial urge for a familiar cultural locale to imbue a sense of belonging in his fictional representation can be reviewed in the perspective of Robert Young. In his essay 'Mental Space', Young observes that 'the most capacious space within which we think about ourselves is called culture' and that 'culture is learned and depends on being brought up within a framework—a cultural space' (2005). It is relevant to mention why Young finds Elvin Hatch's assessment in Adam and Jessica Kuper's *The Social Science Encyclopedia* significant:

> Culture is the way of life of a people. It consists of conventional patterns of thought and behaviour, including values, beliefs, rules of conduct, political organisation, economic activity, and the like, which are passed on from one generation to the next by learning—and not by biological inheritance. The concept of culture is an idea of signal importance, for it provides a set of principles for explaining and understanding human behaviour. It is one of the distinguishing elements of modern social thought, and may be one of the most important achievements of modern social science, and in particular of anthropology. (2005)

Young further notes:

> What is important about the concept of culture which is being developed and cultivated in cultural studies is that culture is seen as lived values or ways of life. This broadens and democratises culture and directs attention to subcultures, so that it embraces the culture of the home, neighbourhood, school, street corner, factory, disco, soap opera, pub, street market, prison, shopping mall, office, profession, seminar or study group, psychoanalytic or psychotherapeutic training institution, country club, college, bingo parlour, transport cafe, cinema, industry, motorway shop and petrol station, singles bar, gay bar, swimming pool, ghetto, motorcycle gang, gym, yoga class, women's or men's

> group—wherever people congregate and act in ways associated with particular activities, values and social relations. Sensitive writers about these and other cultural settings have managed to evoke what is valued and expressed in particular groupings: their rituals, belief systems and the structures and dynamics of their social systems. (2005)

Dehra's old roads, once narrow, have been widened and renovated with urban accessibilities. Although Bond is not against renovation he is aware that the absence of cultural ambience cannot be substituted. He accepts the town's timely advancement, but the loss of childhood memories makes him nostalgic now and then. What is left is memory, which none can take away:

> I wrote *A Handful of Nuts* over a period of three-and-a-half months last winter, when icy winds and occasional snowstorms kept me confined to my small abode in the hills. I felt a longing for the hot languorous summer days of my youth, and in this short novel I tried to recapture something of that time and place. (Bond 1996, x)

A Town of Many Colours: Dehra as a Microcosmic Prototype of India

> One thing is certain. Dehra played an integral part in my development as a writer. More than Shimla, where I did my schooling. More than London, where I lived for nearly four years. More than Delhi, where I spent a number of years. As much as Mussoorie, where I have passed half my life. It must have been the ambience of the place, something about it that suited my temperament. (2008, xiv)

Such is the unfeigned sentiment of Ruskin Bond about his beloved town, which appears as a symbol of belongingness to India. It is certainly the case that this small town, where Bond has spent a significant period of his life, plays a key role in his understanding of his country. He knows Dehra intimately, and the liberating energy of the town rather too well. Therefore, the town's ambience, akin to his temperament, is stronger than any other place which he is acquainted with. Many a time, he has returned to and expressed his fondness for Dehra's laid-back, tolerant, easy-going nature. Dehra has indeed changed over the years but the town's appeal to him still remains the same. Bond, however, does not have to fictionalise Dehra; rather the town keeps appearing naturally in his writing, sometimes as setting, sometimes as character and sometimes both. R.K. Narayan ideated Malgudi to render mood in fiction, while Raja Rao relied on the physical-setting of Kanthapura, a South Indian village in the Kara province, for his 1938 classic *Kanthapura*. Bond's Dehra, which emerges as a site of self-fulfilment is not like fictional Malgudi or physical Kanthapura. It may be closer to Hardy's Wessex, although the tragic grandeur poised through the man-nature conflict in Hardy's novels is replaced here by man's genteel communication with nature, where 'Bond has indeed both humanised and spiritualised' its essence (Singh 1995, 10). Although Dehra is described vividly and sympathetically, it never lacks realism. T.W. Clark and Tarapada Mukherji in their introduction to Bibhutibhushan Bandopadhyay's *Pather Panchali: Song of the Road* remind of that

> [i]n *Pather Panchali* the village is not idealized; it is not explained or commented on; it is presented as it is, objectivity at times, but more often subjectivity, by the people who live in it, and in particular by the two children. There is little formal description. It is not necessary to describe the things one lives with every day; one knows them, as the reader comes to know the village of Nishchindipur, through familiarity. (1999, xii)

We sense almost the same wish reverberating through Bond's Dehra. What further authenticates Bond's setting, besides its geographical existence, is the first-hand experience of the place. His vast knowledge of the daily proceedings of Dehra is ineluctable. But, restricting Dehra merely to a physical setting, the novelist seems to understand, means overlooking some greater vision—the vision that epitomizes Dehra in recollection. In a later period, Mussoorie and Landour replace Dehra as setting, but the old charm never ceases to resound:

> I was just back after four years of living in the West; I had found a publisher in London for my first novel; I was looking for fresh fields and new laurels; and I wanted to prove that I could succeed as a writer with my small home town in India as a base, without having to live in London or Paris or New York. (Bond 2010, 436)

By 'small home town' Bond unmistakably refers to Dehra, which provides the backdrop for human action. In one sense, Dehra is both geographical and visionary; and in the other, even more than the collective both. Dehra, where many of his novels, essays and short stories are set, constitutes 'home' for Bond's fictional identity. In *A Town Called Dehra*, the author-narrator explains:

> The Dehra I knew really fell into three periods. The Dehra of my childhood, staying in my grandmother's house on the old Survey Road (not much left of that bungalow now). The Dehra of my school days, when I would come home for the holidays to stay with my mother and stepfather—a different house on about every visit, right up until the time I left for England. And then the Dehra of my return to India, when I lived on my own in a small flat above Astley Hall, and wrote many of the stories that you find in this book. (2008, vii–ix)

It is this very Astley Hall that served as young Bond's abode after his return and is directly mentioned in *A Handful of Nuts*. Among the stories which are well set in Dehra, *A Handful of Nuts* perhaps remains the most significant because it deepens his connections to space.

Let us try to understand Bond's deepening relationship with the town. Dehradun's etymological connotations tell us that 'Dehra' is derived from 'dera' which refers to 'home', while 'Doon' stands for a valley that lays between the Shivaliks and the Himalayas. Although the novel is not written during his stay in Dehra and appeared much later, it well encapsulates the experiences of the authorial self in a fictional mask. From this sense of belief, he evokes a place, where bicycling with his mate Sitaram, renders the nameless protagonist (manifestly Bond's alter-ego) a revelation. Episodic in structure, this narrative characterises the novelistic transparency in unveiling the plot without unnecessary twists and turns. Thus, far from being enigmatic, *A Handful of Nuts* focuses on life in an Indian town, with the past fusing into the present.

In his foreword to *Kanthapura*, Raja Rao famously notes:

> We, in India, think quickly, we talk quickly, and when we move we move quickly. There must be something in the sun of India that makes us rush and tumble and run on. And our paths are paths interminable [. . .]. We have neither punctuation nor the treacherous 'ats' and 'ons' to brother us—we tell one interminable tale. Episode follows episode, and when our thoughts stop our breath stops, and we move on to another thought. This was and still is the ordinary style of our story-telling. (1974, vi)

Ruskin Bond's decision to choose this 'ordinary' style of story-telling is to delineate ordinary Indian life to make the reader feel how extraordinary it really can be, as to where no Englishness takes part as primal, no colonial hangover undermines the country's traditional values, and no magic realism misleads regularities. Even though Dehradun is neither a 'village' nor fictionalised, the town has a 'rich *sthala-purana*, or legendary history' (Rao 1974, v), linking it to the story of *Ramayana* and *Mahabharata*. The boy-hero's joyous phase while swimming and his camaraderie with the Suswa river gladdens him, and the same rejuvenation among his other characters, too, is reflected upon. The river is said to have originated from the Shivaliks and runs through the Doon valley until it meets the Ganges just above Haridwar:

> There is a little-known legend about the Suswa and its origins, which I have always treasured. It tells us that the Hindu sage, Kasyapa, once gave a great feast to which all the gods were invited. Now Indra, the god of rain, while on his way to the entertainment, happened to meet 60,000 *balkhils* (pygmies) of the Brahmin caste, who were trying in vain to cross a cow's footprint filled with water, to them a vast lake.
>
> The god could not restrain his laughter and scoffed at them. The indignant priests, determined to have their revenge, at once set to work creating a second Indra, who should supplant the reigning god.

> This could be done by means of penance and mortification, in which they preserved, until the sweat flowing from their tiny bodies made the river known as the 'Suswa', or 'flowing waters'.
>
> Indra, alarmed at the effect of these religious exercises, sought the intercession of Brahma, the Creator, through whose good offices he was able to keep his position as the rain god. (2008, 164–65)

Summer in Dehra does not hasten perspiration, it is rather a happy season of mango and the soothsayer of monsoon. The author-narrator's renewed self can sensitise the freshness that rain brings in:

> The mango and litchi trees were washed clean. Sal and shisham shook in the wind. Peepal leaves danced. The roots of the banyan drank up the good rain. The neem gave out its heady fragrance. Squirrels ran for shelter into the embracing branches of Krishna's buttercup. Parrots made merry in the guava groves. (2010, 472–73)

Here mythological Krishna is infused with nature. Such references to Hindu mystification are not uncommon in Bond's writing. It appears that Bond is really moved by Hindu mystification; being particularly influenced by the writings of Sudhin Ghosh (1899–1965)—an autobiographical Bengali writer whom Bond read in Britain and praised extensively. The recurrent motifs of *karma*, of the flute-playing of Lord Krishna, of how integrally human life is entwined with rivers, of transformation with seasonal merriment and of the imagery of baptism through water ascertain his deep faith in Vedanta philosophy. Bond's employment of myth, in fact, emerges from his close association with Hindu philosophy and culture. In the chapter 'Myth as Technique' of *The Twice Born Fiction* (2015), Meenakshi Mukherjee discusses how the employment of myth has become a familiar technique of Indo-Anglian[2] novels. Out of the two different methods of employing myth, Mukherjee notes that (a) 'literary myth' is the direct outcome of the stories from the *Ramayana* and the *Mahabharata*, while (b) the other kind of mythical origin results from local legends, folklore and primitive rituals (127). Before we concentrate on Bond's technique of using myth in this text, it is useful to mention the significance behind this phenomenon, as pointed out by Mukherjee:

> Why are myths important in the study of literature? It is interesting to speculate why poets and writers have always been drawn towards myths and legends. One reason may be their quality of timelessness. Myths, in spite of their distance from contemporary reality, do have, for that particular group of men to whom they are culturally relevant, a kind of fundamental significance. (127)

In this text, Bond's incorporation of myth as digressional method does not, however, fail to permeate 'the collective unconsciousness of the whole nation' (Mukherjee 2015, 129). Bond did not have the opportunity to listen to Indian legendary tales from his grandparents due to a dysfunctional family upbringing. He is acquainted with Indian myths and legends partly from his friends' households and largely through his abiding interest in reading.[3] Nonetheless, the novelist does not wish to restrict Indian sensibility only to legendary connections because he seems to realise that 'weaving in of myths, legends and rituals will not by itself give a novel a special stature unless there is an underlying design holding together all the digressions' and that 'mere description of the rituals will weaken rather than enrich the structure of a modern novel' (Mukherjee 2015, 132). One notices that the climactic point of Holi in *The Room on the Roof*, in spite of playing an important role for Rusty's identity-development, is not exaggerated, lest the novel's primary aim be overshadowed. In *A Handful of Nuts*, the novelist, despite commenting on Rusty's (considering him as the novelist's textual appearance) experiences and love-hate relationship with his nutty friends, prioritises Dehra's daily spectrum.

Bond's Dehra is modern, diverse and liberal, and believes in coexistence. Dehra inspires him for 'a love for all the world' (Bond 2010, 448). The anonymous protagonist, visibly the author-persona, is well at ease both with the church and the *maidan*. Mythology and modernity can live together comfortably. Rusty's musical affinity may be inclined to Nelson Eddy, but he readily admires Indian singers like Saigal and Rafi among others. He describes how Sitaram's jubilation at Talat Mehmood's latest love ballad compels the latter to respond 'with the *Volga Boatmen* in my best Nelson Eddy manner' (449), forcing his landlady to run out of her shop to interrogate their 'cacophony'. Such pluralist assonance between local and global culture is frequently enunciated. A little later, in the text, Bond notes:

> The mango trees were sweet with blossom. 'My love is like a red, red rose,' sang Robbie Burns, while John Clare, another poet of the countryside, declared: 'My love is like a bean-field in blossom.' In India, sweethearts used to meet in the mango-groves at blossom time. They don't do that any more. Mango-groves are no longer private places. Better a dark corner of the Indiana, with Larry Gomes playing old melodies on his piano .... (456)

Unearthing his favourite Dehra, the text seems to suggest what is left unsaid or overlooked in the imperial narrative. The author's delight in recollecting the past—in order to be gladdened by its timelessness, during which his early phase of life bustled and bloomed—can be allied with what French philosopher Rousseau confesses in *Confessions*: 'I see nothing in the future that tempts me; all that can charm me now is to recollect the past, and my recollections of the time of which I speak, as vivid as they are true, often let me live content in the midst of my misfortunes' (221). We can justifiably say that Bond's inclination and bonding with Dehra, which has become synonymous with India, can easily be mapped out from his yearning to restore his formative youth. The novelist firmly believes that India is well resonated in the myriad of experiences of small towns, where poverty, dirt, or material inconveniences do not make one feel isolated, where one barely complains before getting accustomed with the dim-warm light of the kerosene lamp. He indeed proposes that small towns have independent characteristics. Talking about his usual proceedings of life at Bibiji's flat the author-narrator registers:

> I was quite happy cooking up stories, most of them written after dark, by the light of a kerosene lantern. Bibiji hadn't been able to pay the flat's accumulated electricity bills, and as a result the connection had been cut. But this did not bother me. I was quite content to live by candlelight or lamplight. It lent a romantic glow to my writing life. (Bond 2008, x–xi)

Despite her irritation with Edith Clerke, Bibiji[4] allowed the former's son to use her flat. In return, young Bond used to help her with accounts for her grocery store. The author stresses: 'I think it's only in India that you could find such a situation—a young offspring of the Raj, somewhat at odds with his mother and his stepfather, choosing to live with the latter's abandoned first wife!' (ix–x). Bond's biographer, Meena Khorana informs us that '[w]hile Bibiji resented her ex-husband and his Anglo-Indian wife [Bond's mother], she did not blame Ruskin and treated him like a member of the family, preparing his breakfast every morning' (2003, 41–42). One could gauge that while writing in his sixties, Ruskin Bond no longer feels the dilemma of Anglo-Indianness because Indian atmosphere and social connection filter his Englishness. In this novel, Bond's usage of the expression 'offspring of the Raj' should not be considered as an outcome of Anglo-Indian angst but as an affirmation on coexistence and tolerance. Generous Dehra promotes such liberal spirit. Even though the climatic changes, because of excessive deforestation and disorganised urbanisation, disappoint Bond immensely, he welcomes the change as far as the economic progress of the society is concerned: 'We move on, of course. There is no point of hankering after distant pleasures and lost picture palaces. But there's no harm in indulging in a little nostalgia. What is nostalgia, after all, but an attempt to preserve that which was good in the past?' (Bond 2008, 120). Such complacency is not contradictory, but self-affirmative. By fictionalising his own self, the novelist books a free license to accommodate those beaten paths. *A Handful of Nuts* is thus not just a fictional visit, but Bond's own journey to re-experience all that invigorates his self.

Dehra once served as a retiring place for the aristocrat British during the colonial era; the colonial hangover, therefore, was not inconceivable in the late 1940s and 1950s. Nonetheless, Ruskin Bond's Dehra is bereft of colonial overabundance—be it political or social, cultural or psychological. The text is well set in post-independent India that may be attuned to the postcolonial response to colonial encroachment. William Matheson and Jai Shankar are affected by hybrid culture. When the Great Gemini Circus hits the town, engrossing Rusty and Sitaram with its fascinating show, William and Jai, however, refuse to indulge in such popular exhibition. 'They felt,' the author-speaker writes, 'the circus was just a little below their intellectual brows' (Bond 2010, 459). Amidst such high-low binary, it is important to mention how the novelist, renouncing the Western fashion of calling by surname, adopts the tendency of addressing people by their first name. This act also gives the narrator a sense of possession and a close tie with the characters he creates. The inescapable presence of Sitaram becomes alive to us with mere 'Sitaram'; we are not interested to know his family tree. Nowhere, we find the novelist addressing Maharani, Indu, or any other Indian characters with their family names. The representation of Indian values in this novel also finds ample scope through domestic bonding. Dehra, in fact, is embedded in Bond's writing as an interactive setting, whose effect on his characters is so inherent that they can only be imagined in Dehra's genteel presence. Dehra, admittedly, has become an important character in this text.

Celebrating 'Dailiness': An Indian Way of Seeing

'[I]n *A Handful of Nuts* [. . .] I am my usual irreverent self; it is a self-portrait of the author as a sensitive and occasionally mischievous youth. Or rather, of a mischievous elderly author looking back on his innocent youth!' (xii), Ruskin Bond unveils his intention in the introduction to book *Strangers in the Night: Two Novellas* (1996), which includes this present novella along with *The Sensualist*. Bond later confesses, probably in self-defence: 'As a novelist and storyteller I have always drawn upon my memories of places that I have known and lived in over the years. More than most writers, perhaps, I find myself drawing inspiration from the past—my childhood, adolescence, youth, early manhood . . .' (2016, xiii). It is discernible that the novelist is loitering in the world that makes him who he is. Such tendency to retrieve a true sense of being while identifying one's intimacy with a certain space frequently recurs in his writing. As he evokes Dehra's banal spirit, the town, in return, offers a close view of togetherness in his privately built hour.

Behind this evocation thus rests Bond's reclamation of everydayness, where the author-narrator cherishes Dehra's quintessential small-town cosmopolitanism—devoid of city-centric hassle—where life is uncomplicated amidst hardships and failings but proud of ordinary significances. Dehra's middle-class sentiment is caught in the eyes of the 21-year-old protagonist. Sometimes, the author-narrator's lingering eye energises Dehra's slow-paced life with all its curbed resources. Such representation of a particular place is better expressed when one is firmly grounded to the, to what a Bengali would call, *maati/desh* (soil/region), whose vague-but-near English rendering may be 'earth', to denote a spontaneous yet abiding tie with one's true origin, whereupon the innermost emotion is articulated and the process of writing finds satiation. Similar emphasis of subjective investigation is evident in some of Bond's others work too. But, due to the key focus on the developing consciousness of the adolescent-protagonist, where the authorial-identity is slightly younger, there it does not appear to be as strong as it is here. Also, it needs to be noted that the novelist does not unnecessarily romanticise Dehra's regularities; rather Bond's Dehra goes beyond the indistinguishability between living and writing and exists in the convergence between the two.[5] The static nature, if one calls it so considering Bond's reminiscence, is simultaneously living as he is writing. Upon his writing, Dehra's Dehraness is exfoliating. The superannuated appeal of Dehra, I have already stated, is absent in the industrial 'Dehradun' because it fails to align with the novelist's sense of belonging to India. Also, Dehradun's urbanised space does not induce a similar humanistic world because the everyday encounters resulted by 'the memory-inducing makers of space' (Bandyopadhyay 1995, 55) cannot be found in Dehradun and because the sense of rapport with Dehra's sensibilities has lost its credibility in newly-established city-space. There is also a sentimental gap in choosing 'Dehra' over 'Dehradun' because the homely iconography seems to be missing. Dehradun does not engage him as much as the ubiquitous presence of the former. The appeal of Bond's Dehra resides quaintly beyond the din and bustle of city-centric materialism as a kind of locale with a sense of historical grandeur, signifying a direct opposition against everything that perturbs everydayness. It is evident why Ruskin Bond, in his personal life, consciously drifted away with a serious complaint from his favourite town. In this text, 'Dehra', therefore emerges as a sustained critique of what 'Dehradun' with its urbanisation and desolation upholds.

A vignette of private moments studiously nurtured, *A Handful of Nuts* also constructs the author's formative youth and successive camaraderie of the mid-1950s, where the author-narrator's 'underweight' and 'undernourished' body bustled in a street-faced rented room at Astley Hall, with the nipping odour of *neem*-pods from the adjacent pavement. It was a time when his usual day used to begin with *samosas* (an Indian fast food in a triangular shape, usually served at breakfast) or vegetable patties followed by a lunch of rice with *dal* (lentil) and vegetable curry at a small and affordable restaurant called Komal's. Located near Orient Cinema, Komal's catered to limited-budget sustenance and provided him with an easy accessibility to newspapers and magazines at an adjacent newsstand:

> Determined as I was to making a living by writing, I had made it my duty to study every English language publication that found its way

> to Dehra (most of them did), to see which of them published short fiction. A surprisingly large number of magazines did publish short stories; the trouble was, the rates of payment were not very high, the average being about twenty-five rupees a story. (Bond 2010, 428)

Meena Khorana's insight may be read as background reading:

> In spite of Bond's self-deprecating remarks that he was 'lazy', he worked furiously during this time. In order to survive as a writer, he had to lead a disciplined life of regular writing; yet he also felt free because he did not have to conform to the set schedule of a job. He would write for a couple of hours each morning, about a thousand words, then he would go to a café for coffee, meet friends, and eat at cheap roadside *dhabas* ('eating houses') near the Clock Tower or at fashionable restaurants. Upon returning to his room in the evening, he would again write a little. (Khorana 2003, 44)

I have so far discussed why Dehradun's urban space fails to generate the intimacy that the author's autobiographical identity once had with the socioculture space of the 1950s Dehra. It has already been hinted that Bond's kinship with this small-town-sphere is helplessly cut short in the intrusion of city-life lies in its inability to literalise, say, his easy fondness with Sitaram. If the question arises whether Ruskin Bond is nostalgic about his vibrant youth and rendezvous of his 21st-year-vagabond self in his sixties, the author is ready to reveal its significance: '[I]t's often the most significant year in any young person's life. A time for falling in love; a time to set about making your dreams come true; a time to venture forth, to blaze new trails, take risks, do your own thing, follow your star . . .' (Bond 2010, 436). If '[h]omecoming after a sojourn abroad and consequent readjustment and revaluation of the terms in which to face life constitute the major issue in a number of these novels' (74–75) in the 1950s and 1960s, as Meenakshi Mukherjee has observed in *The Twice Born Fiction* while discussing East-West encounter, Ruskin Bond's *A Handful of Nuts*, in a different way, revives the concept.

Ruskin Bond's penchant to see Dehra not as a city but as a town can fairly be answered by what he philosophises in the introduction to *Time Stops at Shamli*: 'Small towns don't change in the way that cities change. It is still possible to find the old landmarks and sometimes the old people. There is a timelessness about small-towns' [Bond 1989, 9]. It is Dehra in the 1950s where William Matheson (of Swiss origin), Larry Gomes (a Goan), the author-narrator (of British descent) and Jai Shankar (an Indian) befriended casually, irrespective of their contradictory notions about life. *A Handful of Nuts* depicts how such mingling, despite veritable differences, is possible in easy familiarity. Here the novelist shows considerable reticence in revealing the idiosyncrasies of his characters, with a subtly detached perspective always ready to amuse and a benign human voice always ready to greet. What verifies the novelist's vision is his treatment of the characters who themselves carry forward the story and make it (un-)eventful.

A Handful of Nuts is a novel of character, which specifies how cultural ambience of a particular space acts behind the dynamics of characterisation. The novelist manages to reveal the passion of his protagonist who, after his return with a dream of becoming an independent English author in India, struggles but survives with determination and heavy workload. The author-narrator, who somehow manages to live by freelancing—a daring profession in the 1950s India, lives in constant fear of monetary constraints. The novel, nonetheless, is not a hero-centric story; here each character is active and visual, and each complementing the other. That Bond is a reliable chronicler of characteristic nuances, may be found at how his characters confess their own traits. Even though the characters are plain, their idiosyncrasies lend dimensions to their commonality. Bond's nonfiction *A Town Called Dehra* informs us that Dehra, at that time, was full of people living on borrowed money. Jai Shankar, the genius of the Doon School, is shown as a semi-comical character in this novel. An ardent *jalebi*-lover, he always borrows money from Rusty to satisfy his appetite. Dehra's coping up with middle-class sentiment is unmistakable here. One notices William Matheson living 'in a posh boarding-house, but always cadging small sums off me [the author-speaker]—to pay his laundry bill or assist in his consumption of Charminar cigarettes [. . .]' (Bond 2010, 431). Suresh Mathur, the only out-of-work lawyer according to the narrator, intends to do something great but is yet to see success. Suresh is almost always badly in need of a drink and discovers 'fourth dimension' at strong bouts. Despite considerable talent in musical understanding, Larry Gomes, a Dehra boy of Goan origin, has to compromise with his musical sense due to lack of scope and economic constraints and therefore rely on a limited salary he gets from the Indiana Hotel for livelihood. Among them, Sitaram, the kindred soul, fills up the freelancer's life with omnipresent intrusion. The narrator also informs us that William and Jay do not trail them (Rusty and Sitaram) to places like Komal's, as it is lowbrow for them. Such a vast array of cross-cultural characters, however, is impossible without an open-eyed spectacle and close intimacy with sociocultural space.

Applause and criticism, however, can simultaneously be put in Bond's manoeuvring of this narrative, in which he seems to be disinterested with plot construction. Bond constantly insists that '[m]y characters were[are] the story' (2015, ix), and that his story relies on close observation of life and emotion. *A Handful of Nuts* in fact whispers, what Henry James in his 1884 essay 'The Art of Fiction' writes as a rebuttal to Sir Walter Besant's emphasis on plot, '[a] novel is in its broadest definition a personal, a direct impression of life' (4). Besides stressing on the 'conscious moral purpose' (4), James maintains that a good novel is impossible from a superficial mind. In this novella with a carefully chosen title, Bond focuses on how characters behave, how their presence lingers on. Bond's characters are lifelike and, since taken from or inspired by real-life acquaintances, compassionate. Thus, we see the narrative wittily humming James's observation: 'What is character but the determination of incident? What is incident but the illustration of character?' (6). Clearly, the novel's credibility multiplies at the author's accomplishment in characterisation.

As we have seen, in *A Handful of Nuts*, the characters briskly run through different corridors of life. It is plausible that Dehra provokes the attitudes of these characters. It is also true that the fictionalisation of Dehra as dialectics of personal space, inescapably engages us to the author's subjective choice, but this, in turn, necessitates an evolving site of identity construction. In Bond's text, the act of returning to pre-urban Dehra is not always faithfully maintained with the progress of the plot. The text, rather, creates a confessional voice. Still, one wonders at Bond's power of evocation and his ability to maintain the equilibrium. The diversifying presence of these characters also engages us to ponder over rich cosmopolitan expression inextricably interwoven in the narrative, and once it is put under critical scrutiny, we witness a modern locale brimming with history. By arguing that the magic of fiction lies in 'apparent resurrection' James Wood, *in an interview with* Peter Conrad introspects that the relevance of a novel is to 'bring people back from the dead on the page, only to kill them a second time—to cast them into the past tense' (2015). Bond's yearning to evoke old Dehra is understandable because of the town's semi-urbanity or small-town sentiment, which comes naturally to his emotional mapping. In this narrative, he is writing about a living space that lingers on in his memory. One may find that this inseparability or failure to disassociate makes it more alluring. At one level, *A Handful of Nuts* speaks quite plainly, with no hair-raising issues of social or political tensions, how these characters meet each other, share lives and depart; at another, it goes on to say chapter by chapter, the characters' active involvement with the space by suggesting an abiding interest of the author to narrate the cultural openness that Dehra possesses. Bond's Dehra is thus open-ended and replete with people across classes and communities, and we notice them celebrating human joy effortlessly. We see the lower-class dhobi's son, Sitaram, roaming around proudly along with 'high-brow' Jay and William. We see local Goan Larry and English superstar Granger on the same plate, while the narrative favouring the former over the Westerner. We also notice characters like G.V. Desani, based on Bond's real-life acquaintance, whose eccentric individuality in sleeping in a coffin is credibly presented. Concurrently, we wonder at the invention of 'Sit-Safe' (fashionably stands for commode), when an anonymous Indian inventor, who claims to have made a unique lavatory-system by putting together Western and Indian formations, requests our novelist to give his creation a suitable title. Indeed, the literary pleasure in Bond's writing seems to emerge slowly but steadily, with an indelible impression of the banal world or non-events. Bond's characters make themselves felt in their own ways. What is further noticeable is that Bond's Dehra is not overweighed by bungalows of the Raj narratives but with commonplace cultural constructs of a developing nation. When The Great Gemini Circus arrives in the town, it lures Sitaram by its grandeur. Such commonplace yet universal image adds reliability to his narration.

All important characters are introduced in the first chapter, and with them, the whole panorama of Dehra is introduced right from the beginning. Bond's characters are infectious; hence none of them is unforgettable. Although some incidents are taken directly from personal life, the novelist warns us not to 'take it [the novel] as straight autobiography' (1996, x). In narrativising the town, the author expresses his urge to reenact his boyish wanderings in order to review his developing relationship with Dehra in particular and with India in general. The text can thus be read like an agency to excavate memory to cognize self, and how it has evolved over the years. The point of argument here is that since it is written in the 1990s, long after his renewing relation with his native place, it appears that the novelist wishes to engage himself with the past to regain certain meaning to life. He could have resisted the impulse of tracing back incidents of superannuated Dehra, but in that case, the verve of the setting would have been compromised. Bond knows his art well; hence he brings back the past as present through the traits and emotions of his characters. Jai Shankar, who wants to become someone in the vein of the French author Andre Gide, is afraid of darkness. He believes in ghosts and always 'in a dither lest he should see the lady [the woman is said to have hanged herself from a mango tree on his way to home] dangling in front of him' (Bond 2010, 432). Jai always needs someone's company until he safely reaches home. Larry Gomes, a versatile piano artist, who can play arrangements from old hits to contemporary tracks, from 'Sweet Rosie O'Grady' to 'Goodnight Irene', with equal flair, has to limit his talent by performing at the fashionable Indiana Hotel for three hundred rupees a month and free meals. Gomes's selection of playing in accordance with his audience's mood is presented with genuine handling and this diversifies the novelist's wakefulness. We are informed about the journalist William Matheson, a Swiss by origin, who has served in the French Foreign Legion before working as an assistant to a German newspaper correspondent, Van Radloff. The character is based on a real-life Switzerland-born journalist of the same name, who came to India as an assistant to Von Hesseltein, working as a correspondent for some German papers. In his book *A Town Called Dehra*, Bond tells us that William is denounced from his job because of his mistake to sleep with Von Hesseltein's wife. In pursuit of a new job, raged William now makes his own fortune:

> William hired an old typewriter and set himself up as a correspondent in his own right, living and working from a room in the Doon Guest House. He bombarded the Swiss and German papers with his articles, but there were very few takers. No one then was really interested in India's five-year plans, or Corbusier's Chandigarh, or the Bhakra-Nangal Dam. (2008, 133)

Despite the fact that nothing significant happens in Dehra, each of the characters is easily identifiable by some quirky trait, leaving an enduring impression of narrative acumen. The Maharani of Magador, the mother of the protagonist's crush, is ready to pounce on young Rusty to fulfil her physical desire. This increases his worry until Sitaram's wise advice helps him escape out of the situation. Suresh Mathur is someone who always wants something strong, and who does not bother with etiquettes while inebriated. In the meantime, we encounter the author's maturing self, who is often found philosophizing life's simple pleasures: 'The night is beautiful, made ugly only by the searing headlights of cars' (Bond 2010, 432). Besides the author's fictional self, the other character who plays a pivotal role in leading the story ahead is Sitaram, a pragmatic Indian boy of sixteen. Sitaram, who lives with his parents in the quarters behind Rusty's rented flat, is a washerman's son. He is 'a skinny boy with large hands, large feet and large ears' and has 'loose sensual lips' (430). Since there is no avoiding of Sitaram, Rusty's camaraderie with the former develops from irritation to affection. Sitaram, a friend in good and bad times, helps in arranging clothes for the narrator's birthday celebration, prescribes curds for his upset stomach, accompanies him on trips, comforts him in existential crises and so on. Right from the early beginnings, Rusty is seen to have consulted with Sitaram in situational crises and the narrative goes on in complete ease in displaying the author-narrator relying on this lower-class Indian: 'We all need one friend in whom to confide—to whom we can confess our misdemeanours, look for sympathy in times of trouble' (478). The novelist's alter-ego confesses that Sitaram fulfils the gap, just as Somi and Kishen in *The Room on the Roof*, Sudheer in *Vagrants in the Valley* (first appeared as *The Young Vagrants* in 1981), and Omar, in real life, in Bishop Cotton School share the same closeness. So when the narrator enquires Sitaram, '[s]o you're going to desert me' (474) at the latter's decision to work at the circus group, we are immediately moved back to *The Room*, where the same sentiment is revealed at Somi and Kishen's departures from Dehra. Companionship in Bond's oeuvre 'is sometimes friendship, sometimes love and sometimes, if we are lucky, both' (Bond 2015, 1). And whenever it results from two kindred souls, it always imparts a strong sense of rootedness. In delineating Sitaram, the novelist shows no interest either in his caste or in his religion; he rather calls him a 'free soul'

(Bond 2010, 480). Bond assures the reader that '[c]aste didn't count for much in a fairly modern town, as Dehra was in those days' (451). Sitaram is someone to whom Rusty can freely express his mind: 'Sitaram made no demands on my intellect. He left me to my writing-pad and typewriter. As a physical presence, he was acceptable and grew more interesting by the day. He ran small errands for me, accompanied me on the bicycle-rides which often took us past the Maharani's house' (454).

It is worthwhile to point out that Rusty's bicycling with Sitaram widens his consciousness. The literalisation of the ride, a seemingly personal import, at once connects him, for example, with the shared fraternity with Somi before his exile. Seen from the present context, this implies a desire to a quotidian reconciliation which, besides maintaining a sense of everyday comfort, takes his suppressed mind away from the thought of present alteration of his beloved small town. Even a cursory glance at certain commonplace nuances, such as the motif of bicycling with Dehra's easy traffic, continues to be an important case study insofar as this is directly connected to Bond's personal impulses when life is less complicated. Such individualistic choice should not be confused with racial politics by which one's taste for greener, quieter, cooler setting is injudiciously linked with such a generalised idea as the British penchant for the Himalayan valleys and tops (Miedema and Miedema 2014, 202). Rather, what is invested in such details is the subjective inclination for Dehra's banal world.

On one such trip, on being asked by Sitaram about his destiny, Rusty replies that he will keep on going anywhere until he feels like going to discover new meanings and directions of life, and in that, we are told, Sitaram would love to guide him, which the narratorial self warmly accepts. As he stops at some secluded canal by a mango grove, the place's collective energy with water, trees, birds, breeze and light rejuvenates his identity:

> A sensation of great peace stole over me. I felt in complete empathy with my surroundings—the gurgle of the canal water, the trees, the

> parrots, the bark of the tree, the warmth of the sun, the softness of the faint breeze, the caterpillar on the grass near my feet, the grass itself, each blade . . . And I knew that if I always remained so close to these things, growing things, the natural world, life would come alive for me, and I would be able to write as long as I lived. (Bond 2010, 442)

This, again, is endowed with his longing to belong to a locale which is less crowded and serene—an agreeable space for self-revelation. As he jumps into the canal's water, the authorial persona, in the tone of reiteration, renews his belongingness to the Indian scene. With his bath, it may be read, he removes the stigma of crossing the black water—the upper-Hindu (mis-)conception connoting that one loses his morale if he crosses oceans or lives in an alien land—and recasts himself as a Dehra-boy.

A passage of revisiting his vagabondage of youth, *A Handful of Nuts* is manifestly a labour of love, where Ruskin Bond triumphs in rediscovering the trodden alleys of human bonding with usual acquaintances. Dehra is, in fact, the result of Bond's embedded psyche so much so that his depressing expatriation fails to wane the years of togetherness. Dehra's realness emerges from the close understanding and cross-cultural cooperation, common to small-town cosmopolitanism. If there is Mr Shankar's New Empire Cinema for English films, Orient Cinema too holds Rusty and Sitaram for hours to provide them with the taste of *desi* films:

> There was filmi music in full measure when we got to the Orient Cinema, where they were showing *Mr and Mrs55* starring Madhubala, who was everybody's heart-throb that year. Sitaram insisted that I return my bicycle and join him in the cheap seats, which I did, almost passing out from the aromatic *beedi* smoke that filled the hall. The Orient had once shown English films, and I remembered seeing an early British comedy, *The Ghost of St. Michael's* (with Will Hay), when I was a boy. (Bond 2010, 446)

Mr. & Mrs. 55, a Guru Dutt directorial, was cinematised in 1955. Interestingly the name of the cinema hall itself entails colonial overbearing, but with the demise of the British in India, the theatre started showing Indian films exclusively when no imperial impositions are left, and when the public taste is changed. The audience used to relish *beedi* (an Indianised version of cigarette), the narrator writes, while watching the sensational Madhubala. In a way, Rusty's narrative performs a dialogic voice, where no authoritarianism is entertained. The Western influence may be strong enough before, but regional proceeding is now ready to replace it. But, far from treating East and West in contesting terms, the narrative focuses on cultural coalescence between the two contradictory poles, retaining Dehra's identical flavour intact. In other words, Dehra is conceptualised beyond the East-West binary.

One of the most engaging and persuasive features of this novel is the employment of comic humour, even though it serves a mere commentary on regular events of the town. Bond's humour is not wry in nature but gentle and wholesome, and occasionally provocative. Let us take the incident of the arrival of the British film star Stewart Granger in the town for shooting a film, which would later be *Harry Black and the Tiger* (1958). Excitement followed at meeting the six feet two inches tall, brown-eyed, middle-aged handsome man, who already had created a stir with his presence against Ava Gardner in *Bhowani Junction* (1956). Rusty chased Mr Granger with his friends of youth and inspected him curiously from the next table at Indiana Hotel. Although Granger came to Dehradun refuting all conjectures, he eventually went away by changing his mind. This allows the author-narrator to make a gentle dig at him, showing his possessiveness about Dehra:

> We heard, later, that they [Granger and his team] had decided to make the film in Mysore, in distant south India.

No wonder it turned out to be a flop. Sorry, Stewart.

> Two months later, Yul Brynner [a Swiss actor] passed through but he didn't cause the same excitement. We were getting used to film stars. His film wasn't made in Dehra, either. They did it in Spain. Another flop. (Bond 2010, 436)

The novelist seems to believe that in order to be truly true to a place, one must have close intimacy with the plentitude of everyday details. Which is why, right from the very beginning, he sets the atmosphere well.

The subplot of the novel presents an unfulfilled love story. The young protagonist is infatuated with a local college girl Indu, whose delicacy is ineluctable and whose playful smile coupled with butterfly gestures allures the freelancer's youthful spirit and swings his heart inside. A middle-class youth's fantasy for his dame is understandably felt in the following lines:

> I dreamt that I was bathing with her in a clear moonlit pool, while small fishes of gold and silver and mother-of-pearl slipped between our thighs. I laved her exquisite little body with the fresh spring water and placed a hibiscus flower between her golden breasts and another behind her ear. I was overcome with lust and threw myself upon her, only to discover that she had turned into a fish with silver scales. (Bond 2010, 430).

Even though the intention of the narrator-speaker towards Indu is 'perfectly honourable' with the hope that 'Indu would give up her protected existence and come and live with me [him] in a house by the sea or a villa on some tropical isle' (445), his towering shyness becomes an impediment to disclose his love. On Sitaram's advice, he invites her to his birthday party with the expectation that their relationship will prosper. Rusty's 21st birthday celebration is basically a disorganised congregation of some ten people with considerable constraints of arrangements. The unavoidable aspect of middle-class commonality is addressed by Sitaram, who by the privilege of being a dhobi's son, can arrange for any pair of trousers out of orders, provided the narrator is not fussy about its owner and returns it timely. In the party, we see Rusty trying to be easy with Maharani, a flabby woman of forty who is described as *Rakshani* (witch-dragon), to remain close to her daughter, Indu. The other day in Indiana, when he meets the woman over a cup of coffee, their meeting is immediately complemented by

Larry Gomes's piano playing 'Love is a Many-Splendoured Thing'. Once Maharani finishes her coffee, Rusty somewhat agrees to her invitation to join her at her house. Meanwhile, suspecting something ominous, Larry Gomes starts playing the 'Funeral March'. This novel, like a few other stories of Bond, abounds in such situational humour, with the narrative slowly taking pleasure in the follies of the central character. However, the news that Indu is hanging out with some handsome prince disheartens our narrator's dream. From the novel's epilogue, however, we learn that Indu is getting married to someone else. This lateralisation of Ruskin Bond's unreciprocated love in real life for Vu-Phuong is hinted to retain the comic sense and dashed hopes of a small town.

Quotidian details, extensively commented upon by Saikat Majumdar while discussing Amit Chaudhuri's fiction, as an important paradigm of cultural knowledge production that has strong historical links with literary contexts (Majumdar 2013, 156–57) generate a ground for discussion in Bond's writing too. It is to be noted that whereas Chaudhuri tends to focus on domesticity at home alone, in Bond's writing domesticity is a little wider, coincided with his known surroundings. Bond's text is not removed from the awareness of ordinary experienced from a personal sense of seeing. Any attention to the text shows that the story, at times, does not proceed at all; thence time stands still in Dehra. Despite the evocative presence of the vast array of characters, there is an inert silence in the text, and through this muteness, the narrator's sharp awareness of Dehra's reality is transferred. This is exactly, I assume, what the novelist's intention is, to hold back the narrative so that the zest of Dehra directly penetrates. Curiously, Bond's narrative does not anticipate anything about Dehra's everyday patterns lest the reader's expectation is shattered; rather it prepares one to ride into a slow-paced life, which in turn acts as a microcosmic representation of Indian small-town spirit. Such revelation is endearing to the reader insofar as it allows him to share a journey with the text. Following the details emanating from the vivacity of street life, the joy in revealing the place's heritage, the understanding of local tastes, and the sympathy in human sensibility, one can safely say that *A Handful of Nuts* literalises a space, where any direct critical enquiry of the East-West binary is ignored by the investment of the mundane. However, the references to Nelson Eddy or Orient Cinema or one's dream of becoming another Andre Gide hardly promote marketability of empire, these regularities rather transcend the limitation of colonial binaries. It is also intriguing to learn which really affects what: are the characters ideated based on the 1950s-Dehra? Or, on the contrary, is Dehra revisited through the characters? Any disclosure of this answer invariably leads us to Bond's sociocultural engagement with the town's regularities.

As is often the case, Bond's works are episodic in structure and largely from his journal entries, which in turn are based on real-life experiences. But, the author has his opinion: 'Life is not a novel; it does not have the organization of a novel. People are not characters in a play; they refuse to conform to the exigencies of a plot or a set of scenes' (Bond 1996, 240). Bond's materialisation of no-plotting may be read as a kind of resistance to foreground 'life' before the narrative. The novel deviates from a proper ending because the novelist's impulse lies elsewhere. Ruskin Bond's ingenuity in describing the present whereabouts of his characters in the epilogue not only shifts the usual novelistic conclusion but suggests his never-ending relationship with Dehra. Dehra may change in the course of time, but the author intends to be loyal to his favourite town. His loyalty can be felt from an emotional response in one of his journals: 'Dear old Dehra: I may stop loving you, but I won't stop loving the days I loved you' (Bond 2012, 656).

At times, the narrative sentimentalises Dehra's timelessness, where the novelist seems to argue that Dehra, to him, becomes more relevant the older it gets. The presence of an objective eye is not always taken care of as Ruskin Bond tends to focus on self-renewing—a motif that recurs in his writing—not merely to justify his belonging to Dehra but to his evolving relationship with the town. It is also true that the transparency of narration does not wholly grant the over-abundance of biographical references, thereby testing the readers' nerves between fact and fiction. But, how often does a writer dare to undertake characters who are basically not anything? This is a great risk undertaken by the novelist. But written in the mature years, *A Handful of Nuts* achieves a likeable originality as the author creates an even atmosphere of small-town sentimentality, avoids decorativeness, accepts human imperfection, celebrates life, castes a semi-comical tone in depicting the characters' obduracy, and manages an inmost view of Dehra, with an emphasis given not upon critical detachment but on authenticity of representation. Dehra, which is a signifier for a home to Bond, simultaneously comingles fictional space and personal space by rendering a sense of familial environ to the authorial self. As a small town, Dehra conveys a vast sense of space, where a struggling writer, a would-be artist, a faltering lawyer and a son of a drunkard dream together. Bond's Dehra is happy to get spacious Rajpur Road that leads life close to the Himalayan top; and curious Daliram bazaar with noise and third-world mediocrity. Here middle-class struggle goes hand in hand with the town's slow-paced traffic, spicy-cheap eateries, occasional power-cuts, easy delight at witnessing the hide-and-seek of flickering light through window panes on dark streets, anxiety over jobs and careers, sundry wishes, aspirations compromised with monetary constraints and the like. Such regular but pulsating vibes amidst all sorts of odds induce a nuanced but genuine idea of a small Indian town, less talked of. The ease in describing Indian middle-class sensibilities could have easily been unmarked at the slightest presence of an outsider. Things might have possibly been defined otherwise, at the stake of sidelining what we have. With each failure, each difficulty, each distinguished struggle, an iconography of everyday India is promised. Clearly, in *A Handful of Nuts,* Dehra suggests a liberal way of conceiving life, departing from the politics of exclusion/inclusion, where the rhetoric of misrepresentation is disallowed straightaway. One, however, notices that Bond's idea of Indianness does not blindly oppose European culture—this should not be taken into consideration on the basis of the author's ancestry—but is observantly filled with an insider's critical eye, before accepting what is good in it. Such eclecticism helps Bond's narrative move towards heterogeneous acceptance.

Notes

1. Dehradun was still called Dehra in the 1950s and 1960s.
2. By Indo-Anglian novel, Meenakshi Mukherjee simply means Indian English Literature or IEL. For more, see M.K. Naik's *A History of Indian English Literature.*
3. In a personal interview, Bond told the author how he was beguiled by Indian legendary tales. In later years, when he spent months in different libraries and in second-hand book shops he read them voraciously. Bond's interest in Indian folktales can be found in *Tales and Legends from India* (1982) and *Indian Folktales Retold* (2015)—the two dedicated volumes on this subject.
4. Bibiji was the first wife of Hari, Bond's stepfather.
5. In his memoir-novel *Friend of My Youth*, Amit Chaudhuri writes:

   > In the meantime, because I'm writing, I'm thinking of Bombay. I think of Ramu. The Ramu I know and the Ramu I'm writing about have become indistinguishable. The same's true of the Bombay I'm recounting from experience and the Bombay I'm assembling through words. This is often how novels begin for me. There's a convergence. I live. Then something prompts me to write. The writing is not *about* life. It is a form of living. The two happen simultaneously. (116–17)

Bibliography

Bandopadhyay, Bibhutibhushan. 1999. *PatherPanchali: Song of the Road*, trans. T.W. Clark and Tarapada Mukherji. Noida: HarperCollins.

Bandyopadhyay, Debashis. 2012. *Locating the Anglo-Indian Self in Ruskin Bond: A Postcolonial Review*. New Delhi: Anthem.

Bond, Ruskin. 1989. *Time Stops at Shamli and Other Stories*. New Delhi: Penguin.

———. 1996. *Rain in the Mountains: Notes from the Himalayas*. New Delhi: Penguin.

———. 2008. *A Town Called Dehra*. New Delhi: Penguin.

———. 2010. 'A Handful of Nuts'. *Classic Ruskin Bond Vol. 1: The Novels*. New Delhi: Penguin, 425–90.

———. 2012. 'Landour Days: A Writer's Journal'. *Classic Ruskin Bond Vol. 2: The Memoirs*. New Delhi: Penguin, 577–675.

———. 2015. *A Book of Simple Living: Brief Notes from the Hills*. New Delhi: Speaking Tiger.

———. 2015. *A Gathering of Friends: My Favourite Stories*. New Delhi: Aleph.

———. 2016. *Upon an Old Wall Dreaming: More of My Favourite Stories and Sketches*. New Delhi: Aleph.

———. 2017. *Small Towns, Big Stories*. New Delhi: Aleph.

Chaudhuri, Amit. 2018. *Friend of My Youth*. Haryana: Penguin.

James, Henry. n.d. 'The Art of Fiction'. *Virgil. Org.*, 1–12. Available at: http://virgil.org/dswo/courses/novel/james-fiction.pdf (accessed on 11 May 2016).

Khair, Tabis. 2015. 'The Cosmopolitanism of Small Towns'. *American Book Review*, 36(6): 4–5. Available at: Project Muse (accessed on 10 January 2017).

Khorana, Meena G. 2003. *The Life and Works of Ruskin Bond*. Westport, CT: Praeger.

Majumdar, Saikat, ed. 2013. *Prose of the World: Modernism and the Banality of Empire*. Hyderabad: Orient BlackSwan.

———. 2015. 'Introduction to Focus: Little India—The Provincial Life of Cosmopolitanism', *American Book Review*, 36(6): 3–4. Available at: Project Muse (accessed on 10 January 2017).

———. 2016. 'Memory and Place: A Conversation with SaikatMajumdar'. Interview by Joseph Daniel Haske, *The Los Angeles Review of Books*, 23 April, n.pag. Available at: https://lareviewofbooks.org/article/memory-place-conversation-saikat-majumdar/ (accessed on 17 October 2016).

Miedema, Virgil and Stephanie Spaid Miedema. 2014. *Mussoorie and Landour: Footprints of the Past*. New Delhi: Rupa.

Mukherjee, Meenakshi. 2015. *The Twice Born Fiction: Themes and Techniques of the Indian Novel in English*. Delhi: Pencraft.

Rao, Raja. 1974. *Kanthapura*. New Delhi: Oxford University Press.

Rousseau, Jean-Jacques. 2000. *Confessions*, trans. Angela Scholar. New York: Oxford University Press.

Singh, Prabhat K., ed. 1995. *The Creative Contours of Ruskin Bond: An Anthology of Critical Writings*. New Delhi: Pencraft Publications.

Truax, Alice. 1999. 'The Allure of the Everyday'. Rev. of *Freedom Song: Three Novels*, by Amit Chaudhuri. *The New York Times*, 28 March, n.pag. Available at: http://www.nytimes.com/books/99/03/28/reviews/990328.28truaxt.html (accessed on 10 May 2015).

Wood, James. 2015. *The Nearest Thing to Life*. London: Jonathan Cape.

———. 2015. 'Literary Critic James Wood'. Interview by Peter Conrad, *The Guardian*, 5 April. Available at: https://www.theguardian.com/books/2015/apr/05/critic-james-wood-religious-view-of-fiction (accessed on 10 May 2016).

Young, Robert. 2005. 'Mental Space'. *The Human Nature Review*, 28 May, n.pag. Available at: http://www.human-nature.com/mental/chap2.html (accessed on 19 May 2016).

6

'The India I Carried with Me'[1]

> Experience is never limited, and it is never complete; it is an immense sensibility, a kind of huge spider-web, of the finest silken threads, suspended in the chamber of consciousness and catching every airborne particle in its tissue. It is the very atmosphere of the mind; and when the mind is imaginative much more when it happens to be that of a man of genius—it takes to itself the faintest hints of life, it converts the very pulses of the air into revelations. (Henry James, *The Art of Fiction*)

Racially an 'Anglo-Indian' in the strictest sense of the term, Ruskin Bond shows no prejudice for Anglicised life overweighing his Indianness in his semi-autobiographical literary endeavours, spanning more than 60 years. An Indian by sensibility, he is frequently questioned about his identity, manifestly because of his British ancestry. Locating him immoderately in the English court and critiquing his work on that basis would, therefore, oversimplify the deep existential angst and the latent desire of an individual who, despite carrying a British bloodline, feels more comfortable in his inherent Indian life. In his oeuvre, as I have tried to argue, the subtle transition from being merely an 'Anglo-Indian' to an 'Indian' is not restricted by Anglo-Indian communal distinctiveness or the idea that an Anglo-Indian is an Indian. It rather liberates the idea of race as being a criterion to determine one's identification. Such fluidity in writing is intimately convoluted with the diverse lives of India and its multitudinous ways of living.

Bond is never ashamed of his double-inheritance. In *Scenes from a Writer's Life* (2012) (henceforth *Scenes* in this chapter) he regards this as a blessing (263). But, more often than not, his desire of simply being an 'Indian' seems to appear as a resistance or, at least, an immediate repartee to spurious jingoism of some questioners, who are blind to Indian colonial history and tend to assess one's inclination towards a holistic identity formation with a set of formulae and try to consign individuals to defined cubby holes. Confusion arises when we fail to realise that an Anglo-Indian, irrespective of his complex origin, belongs to the modern Indian community that is heterogeneous by nature. It is further complicated when we consider him with inherited prejudices and not as an individual who has equal rights as any other citizen of India in post-independent society.

One of the prevailing issues in Bond's works, I have discussed in this book, is to articulate dissension to colonial rhetoric/orthodoxy. In *The Room on the Roof* (2010), for example, John Harrison is the oppositional force against whom an individual will is placed. The novel talks of the Anglo-Indian Rusty, whose propensity to merge into the wider Indian flow, conceives the dialectics of post-1947 Anglo-Indian/national identity. Commenting on the identity-quest of Rusty, Meena G. Khorana calls it 'heroic' (1995, 140) possibly because Bond's 17-year-old-self achieves what most writers of European descent cannot imagine even in their productive phase. Rusty's move from his guardian's restricted world view, we understand, implies the authorial desire to integrate with the post-independent secular way of living. Having realised that Mr Harrison's pro-British attitude will curb individuation, Rusty chooses to depart from the former's monolithic rules. The very idea of such a life-turning move is never easy without a close association with sociocultural reality. The boy's advancement is also significant because his resistance consistently holds against his guardian's Eurocentrism, which could easily have clouded one's consciousness permanently. Edward Said's remark appears to be relevant in this context: 'Western imperialism and Third World nationalism feed off each other, but even at their worst, they are neither monolithic nor deterministic. Besides, culture is not monolithic either, and is not the exclusive property of East or

West, not of small groups of men or women' (1994, xxvii). Had it not been so, the novel would perhaps have compromised the intensity in delineating the tensions of young-adult identity-formation, especially in the colonial aftermath. Rusty is enlightened after his bazaar experience, which helps him declass, at least to himself, all that is rigid, unreasonable and unprogressive. Awakened, Rusty, much like the authorial self in Britain, after his active involvement in the Indian spring carnival of Holi, rationalises the ideas inculcated by his guardian and argues that Dehra's heterogeneous bazaar, which has long been 'forbidden' to him, is more relevant to him than his isolated Anglo-Indian community. Rusty's proverbial slap in retaliation right on his guardian's face and his farewell from the rigid order is a defiance against the colonial instructor in order to proclaim individuation. Not only that, Rusty enacts a direct opposition to the colonial scheme that had once inculcated a sense of superiority in his erstwhile psyche.

The prejudices of Mr Harrison, who appears to be a colonial regulator of the British Raj, is challenged by Rusty and discussed in depth in the third chapter; *A Flight of Pigeons*, discussed in the fourth chapter, interrogates the stereotypes under which Anglo-Indian womanhood/motherhood is trapped. Here we notice a genteel coalescing of class, caste and religion during the colonial regime. Mariam, a mother and someone through whom the central argument is advanced, is of Anglo-Indian lineage. The narrative is however told by her daughter, Ruth, who also acts as narrator-commenter. Mariam shares a close and genuine relationship with her 'Indian' servants who, eventually, become the saviours of her family when the massacre takes place. The key focus of the text is not to justify the mutineers' act as being right or wrong, which the novelist seems to pass onto the reader without any conclusive remark. The novelist neither defends nor condemns the nature of their deeds. That is to say, this should not be read as a decisive choice of Bond in order to keep himself indifferent to Indian history or barricade himself from any categorisation. Rather, Bond's intention here is to display human bonding in colonial Shahjahanpur with a wider scope, which withstands both the prejudiced Raj narratives and conventional nationalist rhetoric. Such resistance seems to reinforce, what Edward Said in *Culture and Imperialism* puts as 'an alternative way of conceiving human history' because, '[i]t is particularly important to see how much this alternative reconception is based on breaking down the barriers between cultures' (1994, 260). Bond's voice, indeed, comes not as a reaction/opposition to colonial history but as an affirmation of human goodness. From the context of the mid-1850s, we move to the setting of the mid-1950s in *A Handful of Nuts* (2010); a leap of some one hundred years, suggests Bond's interest in Indian colonial history.

There is a parallel strain of protest in all of the four major texts discussed here. In the *Scenes*, a direct proposal to and critique of the Anglo-Indian predilection in the 1940s for finding 'home' abroad is issued. The emphasis on the ambivalence of an Anglo-Indian identity is explained in *The Room on the Roof*, the most personal of his works. Here, the resistance to colonial biases, which could blind Anglo-Indian self-identification, is advanced. While in *A Flight of Pigeons* the force of humanism overshadows the dogma of Anglo-Indian womanhood in particular and Anglo-Indian identity in general, in *A Handful of Nuts* a latent investigation to meet his younger self (so as to register self-evolvement) is undertaken. Evidently, the sense of belonging as a part of Dehra's cultural space triggers off the memory-inducing narrative called *A Handful of Nuts*. The appeal of Dehra, where the text is set, is so intense that it once brought him back to India from his self-imposed exile, proffering a microcosmic identity of what conjures up India. How personal Dehra has been to him can better be realised through Rusty's close intimacy with the place and its people.

Once Ruskin Bond's fictional-self distinguishes himself from Dehra's Anglo-Indian ghetto and locates him within a liberal Indian consciousness (which should not be taken as an act of completely disavowing his mixed-blood origin), he owns a sense of freedom. Questions may arise whether the act of identifying everything Indian means a full immersion of Anglo-Indian identity. Ruskin Bond's developing awareness may be compared to what Stuart Hall notes is 'a matter of "becoming" as well as of "being"' (1997, 112). One major issue that complicates such development is race, which, however, is secondary to Bond:

> My own ancestors were not aristocracy. Dad's father came to India as an eighteen-year-old soldier in a Scots Regiments, a contemporary of Kipling's 'Soldiers Three'—Privates Othenis, Mulvaney and Learoyd. He married an orphaned girl who had been brought up on an indigo plantation at Motihari in Bihar. My maternal grandfather worked in the Indian Railways, as a foreman in the railway workshops at some god-forsaken railway junction in central India. He married a statuesque, strong-willed lady who had also grown up in India. Dad was born in the Shahjahanpur military camp; my mother in Karachi [in undivided India]. So although my forbears were, for the most part, European, I was third generation India-born. The expression, 'Anglo-Indian', has come to mean so many things—British settler, Old Koi-Hai, Colonel Curry or Captain Chapatti, or simply Eurasian—that I don't use it very often. Indian is good enough for me. I may have relatives scattered around the world, but I have no great interest in meeting them. My feet are firmly planted in Ganges soil. (2010, 464–65)

Race, as a differential identity, never outdoes the Indianness in Bond's world. His European heritage and identity as a Caucasian or an 'almost white man' become secondary to his long legacy of belonging to and being in India for generations. He and his ancestors for three generations have been Indians either by birth or by sentiment. This dichotomy of race and space brings us across a curious question—what determines the racial identity of an individual: space of birth, the heritage of the community or choice of home space? In his autobiography, published in 2017, the author shares a personal incident in which he was recently denied entrance to the Jagannath Temple in Puri as an Indian (presumably) because of his skin complexion. Though sympathetic to the gatekeeper's ignorance, the octogenarian author reacts strongly against such hasty identification by saying '[i]t is India that has made me':

> Being Indian, and feeling Indian, has little to do with one's place of birth or one's religion. While I was still at school I wasn't particularly conscious of being anything in particular. It was only after I had left India, in 1951, at the age of seventeen, that I realized that I was Indian to the core and could be nothing else. (2017, 276)

Ruskin Bond never writes under the shadow of his British ancestors, and neither do his roots generate racial biases. Reactionary mindsets may consider him half-caste, the orthodox may not see him beyond the territory of his multiracial-ancestry, still others may term him hybrid under postcolonial critical thinking, but Bond's integration with everything Indian is a state of mind—a sense of being, which can hardly be decoded conventionally.

It appears that the mature Bond does not favour the expression 'Anglo-Indian' with regards to his descent; instead, he is so absorbed in his spontaneous choice of Indianness that he rejects his Anglo-Indian communal identity. There is certainly an inspired poetic force, often almost like Henry Derozio, which helps him adhere to his vision. While Derozio's expression lies in his patriotic exaltation, Bond chooses to celebrate the integrity of Indian life. Whereas Derozio is vocal in his love for his country, Bond wishes to be read as a gentle voice of India. What brings them together is the perception of India not as a statutory country for 'Anglo-Indians' but manifestly as a native place of wishes and wants, dreams and anguishes, struggles and aspirations.

'Ruskin's childhood that straddled two cultures and left him orphaned of a father he loved,' perceptively observes Bill Aitken, 'could have produced a bitter adult at home only in the bitching against an unkind fate' (1995, 179). Even though Bond was born with British blood and brought up fairly (but not predominantly) in an atmosphere shaped by European values; his quasi-Indianness, if one is tempted towards any logical reasoning, will eventually fall short of his perspective that recognises India as 'home'. There is no hesitation in it. The reason Bond has remained free of illusions is because his way of seeing, far from being immersed into any set of laws, is never preoccupied. When the mind has no preconceived notions, it endows space to comprehend and to be aware of its surroundings. When the mind is free of prejudices, it obtains a space for intuitive discernment, which consequently leads to spiritual awakening. Such an ability elevates one's perception. When one looks at oneself, Jiddu Krishnamurti reminds us, without any inculcated doctrine, it results in clarity of vision (2006, 54). *Bodh* (comprehension) surfaces from this clarity. Awakened Bond seems to ask in his writing whether Anglo-Indian postcolonial existence (in India) is really possible without an Indian consciousness. In other words, the developing consciousness of the author is such that his multiracial-descent cannot be a limitation. With this awareness not only comes 'freedom from conditioning' (61) but comes *buddhi* (wisdom) that etymologically entails the faculty to comprehend or understand. It is this illuminated mind that never makes Bond conscious or calculative in his identification with Indianness. His approach is rather, what Amit Chaudhuri observes, 'casual' (2001, 414). Chaudhuri perhaps means that Bond's absorption into Indian consciousness is instinctive, not determined by political consciousness.

Noted scholar Mulk Raj Anand compares Bond's outlook to that of an 'insider'. What possibly intrigues Anand more is that Bond's sensibility, much talked upon here, is not detached from local sentiments within the rich composition of Indian culture. Besides calling him a quintessential Garhwali, Anand maintains that Bond's works 'seem to have emerged from within Indian homes' (1995, 34):

> It is not that there were no exceptions among the British writers about India, who entered Indian homes, *bazaars*, interiors of towns and cities beyond cantonments. But, as almost everyone of British writers of the Imperialist period, seldom went beyond the 'Civil Lines' to the 'native' town, they only knew the *Babu*, the Bearer, the *Dhobi*, the *Chaprasi* and others in the servants' quarters of their Bungalows. A few of them had

> shaken hands with the Raja, or Maharaja or Nawab. But seldom had they met the men, women and children in the families and groups of villages, small towns or walled cities. (33–34)

Admittedly, Bond's act of hemming himself in with what we mean by Indian consciousness articulates the fundamental, modern, liberal individuality that Bond's writing boasts of.

Bond's reality is India and his writing never lacks an 'emotional engagement' with his surroundings, which have been conducive to shaping his world view (Khorana 2003, 148). Further, his proclivity for dipping into personal experiences helps him stay rooted in the Indian soil, thereby ameliorating his identity-seeking concerns from the initial psychological anxiety of Anglo-Indianness. It may also be seen as an agency to find a true reflection of his 'self' through fictionalisation. Even though he has to face questions regarding his mixed-blood status, he is free to evince that an Anglo-Indian is also an Indian, and that race can hardly dissemble one's nationality: 'Race did not make me one. Religion did not make me one. But history did. And in the long run, it's history that counts' (Bond 2013, 7). National identification appears stronger than racial identification to Rusty, the author's celebrated self, and therefore his quest for identity seems so convincing. He listens to his heart, undertakes the risk, responds to the intuitive invitation, and prefers the individual call to stale, narrow centrality. By doing so, he emancipates himself from the existential Anglo-Indian question of 'who am I?', which is introduced and intervened as early as in the first novel *The Room on the Roof*, defended in *A Flight of Pigeons*, before arriving at a sound understanding in *A Handful of Nuts*, where the erstwhile dilemma is replaced by an illumination of Indian oneness. If *The Room on the Roof* is the finest articulation of an Anglo-Indian voice travelling from his 'communal' identity to 'national' identity, the later works materialise a symbolic journey simultaneously taken by the authorial persona from (communal) exclusivity towards individuation. Ruskin Bond's self-definition to simply be an 'Indian', therefore, knows no hastiness in decision. He has never been more conscious regarding this; rather, his identification, which reverberates through his semi-autobiographical characters, develops gradually over the years. Once his attachment is deepened with the surroundings, Prabhat K. Singh assesses in his introduction, '[h]is European blood seems to be fully naturalised with the Indian spirit' (1995, 7).

To Rudyard Kipling, Edward Said notes, 'a Sahib is a Sahib, and no amount of friendship or camaraderie can change the rudiments of racial difference' (1994, 162). Ruskin Bond, in the words of Mulk Raj Anand, 'has gone far beyond other British [or the writers of British descent] writers into the heartland without any assumption of superiority and without imposing his own idea of India like other orientalists' (Singh 1995, 8). Whereas Kipling 'had to disown his Indianness to become his concept of the true European' (Nandy 1983, 85), Bond walks in the opposite direction and takes pride in Indian togetherness with his *bodh*. With this, Bond's sense of seeing India develops from a quasi-English viewpoint to an Indian one, from curiosity to belief, from ignorance to illumination, from liminality to an inclusive attitude, from uprootedness to belongingness, from conformity to a liberal world view, from microcosm to macrocosm, from a desire to go home aboard to find home in India, and significantly from self-doubt to self-enunciation. Even if there is a sense of quandary in his approach in the initial works, as younger Bond was indeed interested in resolving his double-identity, in his later works, he writes with a renewal of self-confidence in the Indian context. Since postcolonial Anglo-Indian self-identifications are more fluid and disparate, it is understandable that Bond's developing consciousness with everything Indian is enough for personal fulfilment, where British inheritance is no longer relevant to him.

Note

1. 'The India I Carried with Me', appeared as a section in Bond's book called *The India I Love*, recalls how he could not but see himself as a refugee in Britain and how his return to India eased the very idea of non-belongingness.

Bibliography

Aitken, Bill. 1995. 'When Neighbours Become Good Friends: A Memoir of Ruskin Bond as a Person'. In *The Creative Contours of Ruskin Bond: An Anthology of Critical Writings,* edited by Prabhat K. Singh. New Delhi: Pencraft Publications, 175–81.

Anand, Mulk Raj. 1995. 'Ruskin Bond'. In *The Creative Contours of Ruskin Bond: An Anthology of Critical Writings,* edited by Prabhat K. Singh. New Delhi: Pencraft Publications, 33–35.

Bond, Ruskin. 2010. 'A Handful of Nuts'. *Classic Ruskin Bond Vol. 1: The Novels.* New Delhi: Penguin, 425–90.

———. 2012.'Scenes from a Writer's Life'. *Classic Ruskin Bond Vol. 2: The Memoirs.* Delhi: Penguin Books, 253–404.

———. 2013. 'On Being an Indian'. *A Garland of Memories.* New Delhi: Natraj, 5–7.

———. 2017. *Lone Fox Dancing: My Autobiography.* New Delhi: Speaking Tiger.

Chaudhuri, Amit, ed. 2001. *The Picador Book of Modern Indian Literature.* London: Picador.

Hall, Stuart. 1997. 'Cultural Identity and Diaspora'. In *Contemporary Postcolonial Theory: A Reader,* edited by Padmini Mongia. New Delhi: Oxford University Press, 110–21.

James, Henry. n.d. 'The Art of Fiction'. *Virgil. Org.,* 1–12. Available at: http://virgil.org/dswo/courses/novel/james-fiction.pdf (accessed on 11 May 2016).

Khorana, Meena G. 1995. 'The Two Worlds of Ruskin Bond'. In *The Creative Contours of Ruskin Bond: An Anthology of Critical Writings,* edited by Prabhat K. Singh. New Delhi: Pencraft Publications, 139–41.

———. 2003. *The Life and Works of Ruskin Bond.* Westport, CT: Praeger.

Krishnamurthy, J. 2006. *On Nature and the Environment.* New Delhi: Penguin.

Nandy, Ashis. 1983. *The Intimate Enemy: Loss and Recovery of the Self under Colonialism.* New Delhi: Oxford University Press.

Said, Edward W. 1994. *Culture and Imperialism.* London: Vintage.

Singh, Prabhat K., ed. 1995. *The Creative Contours of Ruskin Bond: An Anthology of Critical Writings.* New Delhi: Pencraft.

Index

Q

R

S

About the Author

Arup Pal is an Assistant Professor of English at Asutosh College, University of Calcutta. He received his PhD from Visva-Bharati University, Santiniketan. Arup's research interests include Anglo-Indian literature, travel literature, popular culture and music. He is currently working on travel literature and city.